Cambridge International

Endorsed f

# Oxford English for Cambridge Primary

# Workbook

# 6

Emma Danihel

OXFORD
UNIVERSITY PRESS

Great Clarendon Street, Oxford, OX2 6DP, United Kingdom

Oxford University Press is a department of the University of Oxford. It furthers the University's objective of excellence in research, scholarship, and education by publishing worldwide. Oxford is a registered trade mark of Oxford University Press in the UK and in certain other countries

British Library Cataloguing in Publication Data
Data available

978-0-19-836634-8

1 3 5 7 9 10 8 6 4 2

MIX
Paper from
responsible sources
FSC® C007785
www.fsc.org

Paper used in the production of this book is a natural, recyclable product made from wood grown in sustainable forests.
The manufacturing process conforms to the environmental regulations of the country of origin.

Printed in Great Britain by Bell and Bain Ltd., Glasgow

**Acknowledgements**

The questions, example answers, marks awarded and/or comments that appear in this book were written by the authors. In examination, the way marks would be awarded to answers like this might be different.

The publishers would like to thank the following for permissions to use their photographs:

**COVER:** Ara rubrogenys / Inmagine.com

**p4**: artshock/Shutterstock; **p5**: chaika/Shutterstock; **p6**: Maryline/Shuttertstock; **p8**: Mansiliya Yury/Shutterstock; **p12**: Mariya Ermolaeva / 123RF; **p13**: Svetlana Chebanova  / 123RF; **p14**: AboliC/Shutterstock; **p18**: K13 ART/Shutterstock; **p26**: Mary Evans Picture Library / Alamy Stock Photo; **p31**: deedl/Shutterstock; **p32**: K13 ART/Shutterstock; **p34**: sharpner/Shutterstock; **p36**: patrimonio designs ltd/Shutterstock; **p39**: Vectomart/Shutterstock; **p38**: ElenaShow/Shutterstock; **p42**: Vaclav Taus/Shutterstock; **p47**: ra2studio/Shutterstock; **p50**: Light-Dew/Shutterstock; **p64**: Jekaterina V/Shutterstock; **p66**: Hein Nouwens/Shutterstock; **p68**: Lorelyn Medina/Shutterstock; **p74**: oguz senoguz/Shutterstock;

Q2A Media Services Pvt. Ltd, Katriona Chapman, Gustavo Mazali, Katri Valkamo, Russ Daff, Giulia Rivolta, OKS Group, Dusan Pavlic, Scott Plumbe

The author and publisher are grateful for permission to reprint the following copyright material:

**John Foster**: `The Price of Fame' and `Summer Storm', copyright © John Foster 2007, from *The Poetry Chest* (OUP, 2007), reprinted by permission of the author.

**Elizabeth Laird**: `Pulling Together' from *Why Dogs Have Black Noses* (Oxford Reading Tree, Myths and Legends, OUP, 2010), copyright © Elizabeth Laird 2010, reprinted by permission of Oxford University Press

**Spike Milligan**: 'The ABC', copyright © Spike Milligan 1963, from *Silly Verse for Kids* (Penguin, 1968), reprinted by permission of Spike Milligan Productions Ltd/ Norma Farnes Management.

Any third party use of this material, outside of this publication, is prohibited. Interested parties should apply to the copyright holders indicated in each case.

Although we have made every effort to trace and contact all copyright holders before publication this has not been possible in all cases. If notified, the publisher will rectify any errors or omissions at the earliest opportunity.

Links to third party websites are provided by Oxford in good faith and for information only. Oxford disclaims any responsibility for the materials contained in any third party website referenced in this work.

# Contents

# We can all be heroes

## Sentence length and the use of 'and'

### Choosing the right connective word

**A** In the following sentences, replace 'and' with a more suitable connective word or words. Try to use a different one each time. Don't forget to add commas where necessary.

1 To get to my cousin's town, I have to first take a bus **and** a train **and** a tram, **and** finally another bus.
2 I drink milk every day at school **and** I don't like it.
3 I don't see my cousins very often **and** we don't know each other very well.
4 I like eating fish **and** I'm very worried about all the over-fishing in the world.

**B** Read this story about a true-life event. No full stops have been used in the extract.

So, Kam and I were completely lost, in the middle of this huge forest and we knew it was bear territory and night time was already falling, so we huddled up together, under a tree to keep warm and then suddenly Kam asked me what that noise was and I said that I didn't know what it was and then she said it was something really big and it sounded like it was coming towards us and I agreed with her and she said that whatever it was, it was getting closer and closer and she was sounding pretty scared by this time and I was beginning to feel a bit worried too I didn't know what to do and then I saw something like two horrible, white eyes coming closer and closer and closer I thought just then I was about to scream and then I saw that it was my dad and big brother, with torches, looking for us.

On a separate piece of paper, rewrite the story using both long and short sentences and extra vocabulary to create tension. Instead of reported speech, use direct speech. Don't forget to use appropriate punctuation.

# Main and subordinate clauses

## Linking clauses to make complex sentences

**A** Choose an appropriate clause from a–f to turn the clauses 1–6 into complete sentences.

**1** This is the girl

**2** I wish I knew

**3** My mum asked me

**4** I was so embarrassed

**5** I will learn to ski

**6** He has known Annul

**a** when I spilt my drink all over myself.

**b** if it snows a lot this winter.

**c** since he was six years old.

**d** whom I was telling you about.

**e** why I had not eaten my lunch.

**f** where I left my keys.

**B** Rewrite the following sentences missing out the subordinating connective and making any necessary changes to the verb.

**1** At the zoo, I saw an elephant, which was eating a banana.

_____

_____

**2** The girl who sat next to me in the exam couldn't find her pencil.

_____

_____

**3** The yellow car, that is parked outside, belongs to my neighbour's son.

_____

_____

**4** I have seen the film, which is showing at the local cinema, three times.

_____

_____

# Using language

## Appropriate language and punctuation

**A** Read this short passage. Add all the missing punctuation to the passage, including exclamation and question marks.

Oh no what was that terrible noise **said** (_____) Omar

There's going to be an avalanche **said** (_____) Daniel

Quick hurry as fast as you can Quicker Quicker Hurry up You must get

to the side away from the avalanche **said** (_____) Omar

I can't I can't make it It's coming too quickly **said** (_____) Daniel

Move **said** (_____) Omar

I'm going too slowly **said** (_____) Daniel Omar I can't… the snow

is … **said** (_____) Daniel

Just do it **said** (_____) Omar Quickly grab hold of my ski pole

I'm aiming for that large rock over there

I've got it I've got it just go go go **said** (_____) Daniel

Made it Wow look at that That's amazing **said**

(_____) Omar A few minutes later Omar gave Daniel a

friendly slap on the back and **said** (_____) It's alright the

danger has passed. Are you OK

Yerr Yerr that was a close one though **said** (_____) Daniel

**B** Cross out the word 'said' and replace it with more descriptive and powerful verbs.

**C** Now write your own dialogue between two people caught in a hurricane together. Try to use really dramatic language to make it exciting and remember to punctuate your dialogue appropriately.

_____

_____

_____

_____

_____

_____

_____

_____

_____

_____

_____

_____

_____

_____

# Word classes

## Past participles

**A**  Write the past participles of the verbs described in the spaces provided.

**1** To jump or spring into the air.                                 l __ __ P __

**2** To pull apart or in pieces by force.                        t __ r __

**3** To transfer or give money for something.              p __ __ d

**4** To work at improving one's knowledge.              s __ __ d __ __ d

**5** To include someone or something.              i __ v __ __ __ e __

**6** Rearrange all the first letters of the past participles above to make another past participle of the verb meaning 'to divide'.                 s __ __ __ t

**B**  Use each of the past participle verbs above in a short paragraph.

_____

_____

_____

**C**  Use the following present participles in the middle of a sentence and then write another sentence using the same present participle at the beginning of a sentence.

*Example:* The dancer came onto the stage, **leaping** high into the air.
            **Leaping** into the air, the deer disappeared into the forest.

**1** limping      **2** crashing      **3** skipping

**1** _____

_____

**2** _____

_____

**3** _____

_____

# Word classes

## A word class wordsquare

Find 34 words in this wordsquare and then write them in the lists around the square, depending on their word class. Some letters have been provided to help you.

| d | s | l | a | m | m | i | n | g | r | i | n |
|---|---|---|---|---|---|---|---|---|---|---|---|
| o | t | i | r | e | d | l | y | l | e | o | a |
| o | u | r | n | o | r | e | b | a | l | n | s |
| r | m | o | o | c | i | n | u | r | u | i | t |
| r | b | u | s | y | e | d | t | i | c | o | i |
| e | l | e | a | p | i | n | g | n | t | n | l |
| h | i | t | i | r | e | d | i | g | a | p | y |
| t | n | i | b | b | l | e | a | d | n | i | y |
| e | g | r | a | b | b | e | d | r | t | t | l |
| h | e | a | l | t | h | y | o | h | l | s | g |
| w | h | i | l | e | s | f | g | o | y | o | u |
| o | v | e | r | p | o | w | e | r | i | n | g |

**prepositions**
i __
__ n
f __ __ __

**verbs**
n __ __ b __ __ __ e
d __ __ __
l __ a __
l __ __ d

**personal pronouns**
__ u __
__ i __
y __ __ __

**coordinating conjunctions**
__ o
b __ __ __

**common nouns**
o __ i __ __ __
d __ __ __
__ __ or
g __ __ __

**adverbs**
n __ __ __ __ __ __ y
r __ __ __ __ __ t __ __ t __ y
t __ __ __ d __ y

**past participles**
h __ __ __
g __ __ __ b __ __ __
t __ __ __ d

**present participles**
s l __ __ __ __ __ __ g
l __ __ __ __ __ __ g
s t __ p __ __ __ __ g
g l __ __ b __ g

**adjectives**
h __ al __ __ __ y
u __ __ y
b __ __ y
ov __ __ p __ w __ __ __ __ __ g

**subordinating connectives**
wh __ __ __ __ __ r
w __ i __ e __
s __ __ __ ce

# Colons and semicolons

## When to use colons and semicolons

**A**  Add the correct punctuation to the following sentences.

**1** A number of children still need to bring in their signed permission slips before they can go on the school trip Hiroto Dana Nathan Abdul Arjun and Teodora

**2** You will need to bring in seven ingredients to make the fairy cakes flour sugar butter eggs milk icing sugar and chocolate buttons

**3** He had a lot of things listed on his birthday wish list a new PC game an art set a book a scooter an mp3 player with earphones and a tin of sweets were just a few of the things he wanted

**B**  Connect the following sentences by using a semicolon and making the appropriate adjustments.

**1** Some people like to eat breakfast as soon as they get up. Other people are unable to eat until they've been awake for a couple of hours.

**2** Many people dislike jogging in the rain and getting wet. Personally I find it very enjoyable.

**3** Leo was extremely cross. He hadn't realised that his brother had left his plate of dinner on the couch where he sat down. Now his new trousers were filthy.

**C**  Write two sentences of your own using a colon.

_____

_____

**Write two sentences of your own using a semicolon.**

_____

_____

# Self-assessment on my learning

## Unit 1 We can all be heroes

Name _____

Date _____

😊 I understand and can do this well.

😐 I understand but I am not confident.

☹ I don't understand and find this difficult.

| Learning objective | 😊 | 😐 | ☹ |
|---|---|---|---|
| **Reading skills** | | | |
| I can begin to show awareness of writers' choices of sentence length and structure. | | | |
| I can identify uses of colons and semi-colons. | | | |
| I can identify different word classes. | | | |
| **Writing skills** | | | |
| I have developed grammatical control of complex sentences. | | | |
| I can punctuate speech and use apostrophes accurately. | | | |
| I can plan a plot, describe characters and structure a narrative successfully. | | | |
| I can use a wide range of connectives to make complex sentences. | | | |
| I can identify the main clause and other clauses in a complex sentence. | | | |
| I can use punctuation effectively to mark out the meaning in complex sentences. | | | |
| I can punctuate speech and use apostrophes accurately. | | | |
| I can develop some imaginative detail through careful use of vocabulary. | | | |

I would like more help with _____

_____

_____

# Health and sport

## Using the right words

**Read this article from a school newspaper.**

Perhaps one of the most naturally gifted athletes the world has ever seen and regarded as the fastest man on earth ever, Usain Bolt, nicknamed `Lightning Bolt', recently confirmed his unique talent by winning Gold in 100m, 200m and the 4x100m at the 2015 World Championships in Beijing.

Usain Bolt was born on the 21st August 1986 in Jamaica, where he grew up. As a young child, he spent most of his time playing cricket and football. He discovered a talent for running when he started school but it took a while before he took his talent seriously. By the age of 15, the young Usain was nearly 2 metres in height and he completely dominated the 2002 World Junior Championships. He was the youngest person ever to win the 200m race and was a member of the teams who set a new record in the 4x100m relay and the 4x400m relay. At the age of 17, he signed his first professional contract. At the 2003 CARIFTA games, he won gold medals, but a leg injury didn't allow Usain to perform well in the 2004 summer games in Athens. By 2007, he was recovered and won Silver at the World Championships. But it was at the Olympics in 2008 that Usain Bolt became a household name.

Usain Bolt took the 2008 Olympics in Beijing by storm. He won 3 gold medals and broke 3 world records. He became the first man in history to win both the 100m and 200m races in world record times; and was also part of the 4x100m team that smashed that world record.

He maintained his legendary status in the 2012 Olympic Games in London by defending all three of his Olympic titles and again being part of the team that set a new world record in the 4x100m relay.

In the 2015 World Championships in Beijing, Usain Bolt one again proved what a legend he is. Despite a year hampered by injury, he delighted the world by once again defending all three of his titles.

Usain Bolt says he will retire from athletics after the 2017 World Championships in London. The 28-year-old six-time Olympic gold medallist says that he will focus on just one race in 2017 - the 100m. Bolt had hinted that the Rio Games in 2016 would be his last major championship but he now says he will retire after the London Games.

## A Comprehension

**1** What name is Usain popularly given?

_____

**2** How did Usain `dominate' the 2002 World Junior Olympics?

_____

**3** Why was it quite surprising that he did so well in the 2015 games?

_____

## B Using information from the text, answer the following questions.

**1** Match each of the subheadings below with one of the paragraphs in the text.
**Legendary status**     **Lightning Bolt!**     **The future**     **Growing up**

_____

**2** What is the purpose of subheadings in a text like this?

_____

**3** This text is a short biography. List five general features of a biography.

_____

_____

## C

**1** Find a synonym for the following words in the first paragraph of the text.

thought of _____ exclusive _____ talented _____

**2** Usain Bolt <u>took</u> the 2008 Olympics <u>by storm</u>. To take something 'by storm' is an idiom. Explain what it means.

_____

_____

**3** Research a sports person you admire and/or is popular in your country. Write a short biography of them. Say when and where they were born and grew up. What they have achieved so far and what they want to achieve in the future.

Please use a separate sheet of paper.

# Connectives

## Connectives used to change topics and put points in order

**A** Complete the following dialogue by choosing one of the connectives below.

**although    yet    on the other hand    but    however    though**

Kim:     Hi, Lee. What do you want to do tomorrow?

Lee:     Hi, Kim. Well, we could go to the outdoor swimming pool.
_____, I heard it might rain tomorrow. _____ we
could always go to the indoor swimming pool _____ that
is, of course, rather expensive _____ not as expensive
as going to the cinema. The cinema is the most expensive option
_____ I do enjoy going there the most. _____
it would also be a shame to be inside if the weather turns out to
be nice. I don't know what to do tomorrow!

Kim:     Grrr, I give up.

**B** Complete this list of instructions by choosing one of the connectives below.

**firstly    secondly    next    finally    after that    after    then**

_____ measure the butter and put in a large dish. _____
add the sugar and _____ beat together
with a wooden spoon. _____ a few minutes
the mixture should be creamy. _____ add the
eggs, one by one, and continue mixing. _____
carefully fold in the flour. _____ put the
mixture into a tin and bake in the oven for 35 minutes.

# More connectives

## Connectives used to add points and to explain a point

 **Complete the following letter by choosing one of the connectives below.**

**for a start    furthermore    and    moreover    in addition    for example**

I am writing to complain about the terrible service that I received at your fast food restaurant last Friday evening. _____ the table that we sat at was filthy _____ no one came to clear it. _____ there were bits of food and old, greasy burger papers littered all over it. _____ we then had to wait fifteen minutes for someone to take our orders and, _____ another twenty minutes before the food was served to us. _____ to add insult to injury, when the food finally arrived, it was cold! I will not be returning for a second visit.

**B** **Complete the following sentences by choosing one of the connectives below.**

**similarly    therefore    this shows    for example    this means that**

I am extremely particular about what I eat. _____
I don't eat any meat, fish, potato, onions, flour, wheat products, or milk products. _____ it is very difficult to eat out at a restaurant. _____ it is equally difficult to go around a friend's house for dinner. _____ I usually have to stay in every night and eat by myself. _____ that it's not a lot of fun having a very limited diet!

# Prefixes and suffixes

## Defining words

 **A** Match the words (1–5) using a prefix or a suffix, below, with their definitions (a–e).

**1** meaning**ful**          **a** ancestor

**2** **un**pack             **b** full of significance, purpose or value

**3** **re**form             **c** to understand incorrectly

**4** **mis**interpret        **d** to undo or remove the contents

**5** **fore**father          **e** to form again

**B** Choose a root word from the list below, then add a prefix or a suffix from the clouds. Now match the new word to its definition below.

cover       help       colour

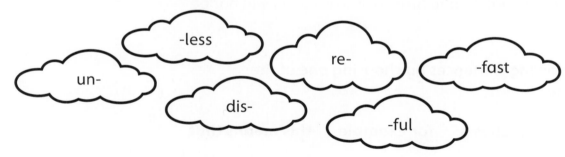

**1** giving aid or service to _____

**2** to reveal, disclose or show something _____

**3** (fabric) having a colour that does not change when washed _____

**4** without colour _____

**5** weak, having no power or strength _____

**6** to get well after an illness, or to find again _____

**7** to find something new, or to learn for the first time _____

**8** having intense or varied colours _____

# Simple, compound and complex sentences

## Working with different kinds of sentence

**A** **Complete these simple sentences with an appropriate finite verb.**

**1** I _____ my toes lightly in the cool, shimmering water.

**2** It _____ great news!

**3** She _____ the book on the table.

**4** Yesterday, they _____ on holiday for two weeks.

**B** **Decide whether the following sentences are simple, compound or complex.**

**1** I like Eddy, but sometimes he's a bit silly.

_____

**2** It's quite late, so if you want to get up early, you should go to bed now.

_____

**3** The six beautiful, brown and black hens in the garden lay an egg each, every day.

_____

**C** **Write three sentences about what you will do tomorrow. Make one simple sentence, one compound sentence and one complex sentence.**

Simple _____

Compound _____

_____

Complex _____

_____

# Modals

Modal verbs are used to indicate how sure the writer is that something happened, is happening or will happen, using verbs like could, might, or will.

## Which is the right modal to use?

**A** Complete these sentences about yourself.

1 If I were older, I might _____

2 If I were much taller, I could _____

3 If I were very rich, I could _____

4 If I were a bird, I would _____

**B** Complete these sentences with a suitable modal verb.

**must     might     can't     would     can**

1 You _____ go in there because it's not allowed.

2 She said she _____ definitely play tennis with me, when it stopped raining.

3 _____ I borrow a pencil please? I've lost mine.

4 There are a lot of clouds building up so it _____ rain this afternoon.

5 You _____ wipe your shoes or you will not be allowed in.

**C** Write your own sentences using the following modal verbs.

won't_____

will_____

should_____

shall_____

cannot_____

# Self-assessment on my learning

## Unit 2  Health and sport

Name _____

Date _____

😊 I understand and can do this well.

😐 I understand but I am not confident.

☹ I don't understand and find this difficult.

| Learning objective | 😊 | 😐 | ☹ |
|---|---|---|---|
| **Reading skills** | | | |
| I can recognise the key features of biographies. | | | |
| I can compare the language the style of biographies. | | | |
| I can create a biography about someone. | | | |
| **Writing skills** | | | |
| I can use prefixes and suffixes in my writing. | | | |
| I can write simple, compound and complex sentences. | | | |
| I know how to select appropriate styles of non-fiction to influence my own writing. | | | |
| I can use connectives in my writing. | | | |
| I can use modals in my writing. | | | |

I would like more help with _____

_____

_____

_____

# Stormy weather

## Summer storm

Light travels, said Miss,
Faster than sound.
Next time there's a storm,
When you see the lightening,
Start counting slowly in seconds.
If you divide
The number of seconds by three,
It will tell you
How many kilometres you are
From the centre of the storm.

Two nights later,
I was woken
By the lashing rain,
The lightening,
And the thunder's crash.

I lay,
Huddled beneath the sheet,
As the rain poured down
And lightening lit up the bedroom,
Slowly counting the seconds,
Listening for the thunder
And calculating the distance
As the storm closed in –

Until,
With a blinding flash
And a simultaneous ear-splitting crash,
The storm passed
Directly overhead.
And I shook with fright
As the storm passed on,
Leaving the branches shuddering
And the leaves weeping.

*John Foster*

# Comprehension

**A**   **Use words and phrases from the poem to support your answer.**

**1** Who is speaking in the poem?

_____

**2** What is the speaker trying to calculate in the poem?

_____

**3** Read verse 4 again. What was it about the storm that frightened the speaker so much?

_____

_____

**1** How does the poet build up the tension?

_____

_____

**2** The writer used rhyme in only one place in the poem. What effect does this have?

_____

_____

**1** What figurative technique has the poet used in the last two lines of the poem?

- Alliteration
- Metaphor
- Simile
- Personification

_____

**2** What effect has the poet created by using this imagery at the end of poem?

_____

_____

# Vocabulary

 **Put these adverbs describing how someone speaks into the correct box. Some words might go in more than one box.**

sob, whisper, scream, sheik, titter, whimper, mutter, murmur, mumble, lament, giggle, bawl, howl, chuckle, sigh, whimper, bellow, screech, blubber, weep, roar, wail, grin, bark, hushed, snivel

| quietly | loudly | happily | sadly |
|---------|--------|---------|-------|
|         |        |         |       |
|         |        |         |       |
|         |        |         |       |
|         |        |         |       |
|         |        |         |       |

# Reading and writing

 **Read this summary of the opening of the play _Twelfth Night_.**

Off the coast of Illyria, a terrible storm causes a passing ship to hit rocks and sink. Inside his palace, Duke Orsino is pining for the woman he loves – Lady Olivia. Alas, she is mourning her dead brother and does not return his love. Meanwhile, a beautiful, young, woman named Viola is swept from the sunken ship to the shore of Illyria. Finding herself alone in a strange land and believing that her twin brother, Sebastian, must have drowned when the boat sunk, she realises that to survive she needs to work. To make this easier, she decides to disguise herself as a man. She changes her name to Cesario, and goes to work in the household of Duke Orsino.

1  **You are the director of a play – _Twelfth Night_. Your actors have asked you to describe the characters they are playing. Using the summary and your own ideas describe <u>one</u> of the characters.**

Name: _____

Age: _____

Appearance: _____

Personality: _____

Emotions: _____

**2** Write your own dialogue between two of the characters, expressing their feelings and emotions. Try to use really dramatic language. Remember to punctuate your dialogue appropriately.

_____

_____

_____

_____

_____

_____

_____

_____

**C** Write a short playscript with two siblings having an argument about the toys they are playing with. Use words from the columns above to describe how they speak to each other.

# Writing a playscript

## Kam in the forest

 Look at the story on page 4 about the writer and Kam in the forest. Change the story into a short playscript with directions for the place where it happens, lighting, background noise as well as the dialogue, and how it should be spoken. Extend the story to the dialogue between the father, brother, Kam, and the writer when they all meet in the forest.

**It might start something like:**

Two children sit huddled together under a tree in a deep forest. Night time is approaching so it is already dark.

Kam:  What's that noise? [*in a frightened whisper*]

_____

_____

_____

_____

_____

_____

_____

_____

# Poetry comprehension
## Windy Nights

Whenever the moon and stars are set,
Whenever the wind is high,
All night long in the dark and wet,
A man goes riding by.
Late in the night when the fires are out,
Why does he gallop and gallop about?

Whenever the trees are crying aloud,
And ships are tossed at sea,
By, on the highway, low and loud,
By at the gallop goes he.
By at the gallop he goes, and then
By he comes back at the gallop again.

*Robert Louis Stevenson*

**A** **Use words and phrases from the poem to support your answers.**

**1** How does the poet create action and rhythm?

_____

_____

**2** Look at the last word in each line of the poem. Write a list of the pairs of rhyming words the poet has used.

_____

_____

**3** How does the writer use imagery to paint a picture of the weather?

_____

_____

# Hamlet

**Here is the opening scene from a play by William Shakespeare called *Hamlet*.**

The snow fell heavily and Hamlet was freezing cold as he pulled his cloak up around him, a thin veil against the icy, bitter chill. He had his eyes fixed on the spot where the guards had told him they had seen his father's ghost the night before. His best and oldest friend, Horatio, was with him.

The bells announcing midnight rang out all around them. At the last stroke of midnight, Hamlet saw the snowflakes swirl around in a wild frenzy and take on the figure of his father - and saw the figure beckoning him to go to him. Horatio begged Hamlet to be cautious but Hamlet ignored him. He ran through the heavy snow, his heart pounding, and called to his father, asking him why he had appeared. The ghost was dressed in armour. The face of his father was pale and twisted in anguish. His voice, was a groan of despair.

To Hamlet's utter horror the ghost explained to him that his own brother, Hamlet's uncle, had murdered him. That as he slept in a sun-filled orchard his brother had crept upon him and put poison in his ear. Hamlet couldn't believe what he was hearing. His uncle had murdered his father. His uncle had stolen his father's throne and now his father's ghost was telling him that he could not rest until Hamlet avenged his murder. Before he could make any response, the ghost faded away into the snowy darkness, the echoes of his voice lost in the howling wind. Horatio ran up to Hamlet and asked him what had happened. Hamlet was speechless though, unable to make any reply. Worried about his friend, Horatio gently led Hamlet back inside.

 **Turn the scene into a short playscript.**

Use a separate sheet of paper.
Check the list of success criteria below to help you.

| | |
|---|---|
| I have introduced and described the setting. | I have put the characters names on the left. |
| I have put a colon after the characters names. | I have started a new line every time a new speaker speaks. |
| I have put my stage directions in brackets. | I have put my stage directions in the present tense. |
| I have stage directions for how the actors speak. | I have stage directions for how the actors move. |
| I have used capital letters to emphasise words. | I have NOT used speech marks. |

# Self-assessment on my learning

## Unit 3 Stormy weather

Name _____

Date _____

😊 I understand and can do this well.

😐 I understand but I am not confident.

☹ I don't understand and find this difficult.

| Learning objective | 😊 | 😐 | ☹ |
|---|---|---|---|
| **Reading skills** | | | |
| I have developed familiarity with an established author – Shakespeare. | | | |
| I can comment on a writer's use of language. | | | |
| I can explore figurative language. | | | |
| I can analyse the success of poems in evoking a particular mood. | | | |
| I can read and interpret poems in which meaning is multi-layered. | | | |
| **Writing skills** | | | |
| I can develop some imaginative detail through careful use of vocabulary. | | | |
| I can adapt the conventions of a text type for a particular purpose i.e. to write a playscript. | | | |

I would like more help with _____

_____

_____

_____

# Traditional tales and fables

## Vocabulary

**Read this traditional tale from South America.**

In the Andes Mountains of Ecuador there once lived two <u>fast</u> friends, the Clouds and Forest. They were such good friends that they would be completely <u>absorbed</u> by each other for weeks and weeks on end. One day however, they had a <u>squabble</u>, which turned into rather an unpleasant ruckus and soon got completely **out of hand**. There was such an air of hostility between the old friends and neither would **back down**. The Clouds decided to go somewhere else and Forest decided to focus on expanding its size.

But the animals and birds of the forest were miserable that the two friends had **fallen out** because their lives depended on the Clouds and Forest being together. They thought of a <u>cunning</u> plan **to get** the two friends **back together**. The great condor wrote a <u>charming</u> apology letter and flew to the Clouds with it saying it was from the Forest. Meanwhile, the anaconda gave a copy of the same letter to the Forest, but signed it from the Clouds. However, neither the Clouds nor Forest were fooled by the letters. They both **saw through** the trick straight away and <u>scolded</u> the animals severely.

Seeing their plan fail, the unhappy animals and birds prepared to leave the forest and look for somewhere else to live. That night the forest was very quiet. But the next morning all the animals were really surprised to see the Cloud and Forest had **got back** together, acting as if nothing had ever **come between** them. Surprised, the condor, anaconda and other animals went and asked the two friends why they had **made up** again. With a smile, the friends explained - your letters made us realise just how well we know each other and also what our friendship means, not just to us, but also to others around us.

**28**

**A** Comprehension

**1** Who were such good friends?

_____

**2** What happened that made them stop being friends?

_____

**3** Who was affected by the breakup of their friendship?

_____

**4** How did those who were affected by the end of the friendship, try to get the friends to be friendly to each other again?

_____

**5** Choose the best moral for this story.

   **a**   Think about others before you think about yourself.

   **b**   True friends are hard to find so when you find them, keep them.

   **c**   Treat others as you want to be treated yourself.

   **d**   True friends don't fall out with each other.

**B**

**1** In the text, some of the words are underlined. Match these words with a syonym listed below.

disagreement _____ lovely _____ great _____

clever _____ taken up _____ tell off _____

**2** Explain what **out of hand** means (line 8).

_____

**C** **Find the following phrasal verbs in the text and use the context in which they are used, to explain their meaning.**

● to make up _____

● to see through _____

● to back down _____

● to fall out _____

● to get back together _____

# Homophones

## Same sound, different spelling!

**A** Complete these sentences by putting the correct homophone in each of the gaps.

1 In the _____ (past/passed) young people _____ (past/passed) their driving licences without having to take a theory test.

2 I don't know _____ (whether/weather) the _____ (whether/weather) will be good or bad tomorrow.

3 You are not _____ (aloud/allowed) to play your music _____ (aloud/allowed) in the library because it might disturb others.

4 Her mother (new/knew) _____ that Cecilia would just love her _____ (new/knew) dress.

**B** Find a homophone of the underlined word in the following sentences and write a new sentence using the homophone. The first one has been done for you.

1 Her <u>waist</u> is so narrow I can almost fit my hands around it. Don't throw so much food away — it is such a <u>waste</u>.

2 Next <u>week</u> I am going to start my tennis lessons.

_____

3 She picked her mother a beautiful <u>flower</u> to say 'thank you'.

_____

4 Don't forget to <u>write</u> me a message when you are on your holiday.

_____

**C**

1 Write down the homophones of the following words.

plain _____  blue _____  red _____  bury _____  bean _____

aunt _____  threw _____  hole _____  stairs _____  see _____

higher _____  waste _____  poor _____  sight _____  peace _____

2 Choose four of the homophones above and put each one into a sentence. Use a separate sheet of paper.

# Using adjectives

## Putting adjectives into the right order

If you are using more than one adjective to describe a noun, then there is a specific order.

**The order is:**

1st **opinion** (e.g. wonderful), 2nd **size**, (e.g. small), 3rd **age** (e.g. old), 4th **shape**. (e.g. rectangular), 5th **colour** (e.g. yellow) 6th **origin**. (e.g. Japanese), 7th **material**. (e.g. steel)

*Example:* A wonderful, small, old, rectangular, yellow, Japanese, steel car.

**A**  Put the adjectives in brackets in the correct order to describe the noun.

**1** a tree (golden, beautiful, tall) _____

**2** a cat (ginger, old, smelly, big) _____

**3** a skyscraper (glass, cool, modern) _____

**4** a plate (plastic, large, round) _____

**5** a hat (blue, woolly, comfortable, old) _____

**B**  Write three or four adjectives to describe the following nouns. (Note: it is not common to use more than three adjectives to describe a noun.)

a drink _____     a horse _____

a friend _____     a book _____

a pair of socks _____     a dolphin _____

**C**  Write three sentences and use appropriate adjectives to describe a forest as if it is a) a terrible and frightening place to be b) a beautiful and peaceful place to be and c) a magical place to be.

**a** _____

_____

**b** _____

_____

**c** _____

_____

# Modals

**Modal verbs are used to show possibility, ability, obligation or permission.**

**Possibility**: modal verb can be used to show how likely something is to happen, using verbs like might, could or will. .

**Ability**: modal verbs can be used to show someone's ability to do something using words like can or could.

**Obligation and advice**: modal verbs can be used to show something is necessary or compulsory, to give instruction or advice.

**Permission:** modal verbs are used to ask for and give permission.

**A** What is the purpose of the modal verbs in these sentences? To state possibility, ability, obligation? Or to give advice or permission?

**1** You must finish your work before you go out to play.

_____

**2** If we work quickly, we might get extra playtime today.

_____

**3** I've completed my work; may I leave the table now?

_____

**4** It's so cold today. You should put a coat on if you're playing outside.

_____

**B** Complete these sentences with a suitable modal verb.

should    may    might    could    can't    shouldn't    must    can    have

**1** If the fire alarm goes off, everybody _____ leave the classroom.

**2** You _____ do some form of regular exercise each week.

**3** I _____ run very fast but I _____ run for a very long time.

**4** If I go to university, I _____ study medicine or I _____ even study to be a vet.

**C** Complete the following sentences with your own ideas.

**1** When I visit him, my grandad will _____

**2** With my pocket money, I could _____

# Conditional sentences

**A** **Complete these sentences with a clause containing *will*/*might*.**

**1** If I go on holiday this year, _____

**2** If the weather is nice this weekend, _____

**3** If I save enough money, _____

**4** When I am a teenager, _____

**5** When I have finished studying, _____

**B** **Make your own conditional sentences using *would*/*could* and the following words.**

**1** Play, instrument

_____

**2** Everybody, tolerant

_____

**3** Rule, world

_____

**4** No ice, Arctic

_____

**5** Money, world

_____

**C** **Rewrite these sentences using *if only*.**

**1** I wish I didn't have to go to my cousin's wedding.

_____

**2** I wish I had been given the game I wanted for my birthday.

_____

**3** I wish my meal wasn't so spicy.

_____

# Active and passive

## Switching between active and passive

**A** Decide which of these sentences are passive and which are active. Circle 'A' or 'P' to give your answer. Then rewrite active sentences as passive and passive sentences as active in the space below.

**1** Friends and family celebrated a great-grandmother's 121st birthday, last week. A/P

_____

**2** A teenage boy is given permission by his head teacher to paint his school red. A/P

_____

**3** A complete mammoth skeleton has been found by a boy in melting ice in Russia. A/P

_____

**4** A woman offers a large reward for the return of her missing suitcase. A/P

_____

**5** A giant shoal of blue whales is seen by holiday makers off the coast of Valencia. A/P

_____

**6** A girl of five was saved by a zookeeper from a tiger's cage in a zoo in Bangladesh. A/P

_____

**B** Finish these sentences with a passive verb.

*Example:* **A pot of gold** was found in the cellar of a deserted, old house.

**1** A box of valuable jewels _____

**2** A group of school children _____

**3** The tiger _____

**4** Apples _____

**5** A lot of food _____

# Self-assessment on my learning

## Unit 4 Traditional tales and fables

Name _____

Date _____

😊 I understand and can do this well.

😐 I understand but I am not confident.

☹ I don't understand and find this difficult.

| Learning objective | 😊 | 😐 | ☹ |
|---|---|---|---|
| **Reading skills** | | | |
| I can use different types of words like adjectives correctly. | | | |
| I can use model verbs successfully. | | | |
| I can answer questions based on information in a text. | | | |
| I understand how connectives are formed. | | | |
| I can use active and passive verbs in a sentence. | | | |
| **Writing skills** | | | |
| I can choose the correct spelling of homophones. I can use the style of the text as a model for my own writing. | | | |

I would like more help with _____

_____

_____

_____

# 5  School days

## Persuasive text

### Writing to convince

**A** Read these advertising slogans (1–6) and match them to the product they are selling (a–f).

1 Nothing comes between me and my Calvins!    **a** dog food

2 Make yourself heard!    **b** bottled water

3 Freshly squeezed glaciers    **c** a car

4 Doesn't your dog deserve it?    **d** a mobile phone company

5 The ultimate driving machine    **e** a playstation

6 Fun anyone?    **f** jeans

**B** Read the advert below for *Manic Mania*, a PC game, then complete the text by filling the gaps with one of these adverbs or adjectives.

**brilliant   extreme   intense   amazingly   sensational**
**grippingly   fabulous   electrifying   thrilling   awesome**

Get ready for the most _____ adventure of your life.

Based on the classic Manic game, *Manic Mania*, the most _____ fast

and _____ manic ride so far races on to your PC.

Six new _____ characters race at _____ speed. With such

_____ graphics and _____ new customised supercars –

this will be the most _____, the most _____, the most

_____ ride you'll ever want to go on.

Have you got what it takes? Then prepare to be blown away.

**C** Match the words taken from the advert in exercise B with their definitions.

Circle the two words which are synonyms.

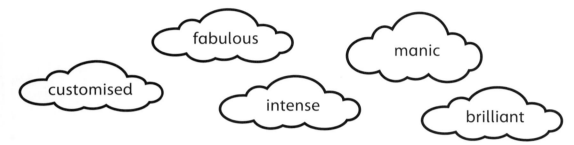

**1** extremely good _____

**2** to build to individual or personal preference _____

**3** desperate or wild with excitement or fear _____

**4** serious, extreme _____

**5** very impressive _____

# Using the right connective

## Choose the right word

**A**    Put the correct connective into the gaps below.

**consequently**    **especially**    **finally**    **as soon as**    **next**
**despite**          **however**       **because**

Agnes was sitting in her seat waiting for the circus to begin.

_____ the curtain went up and there was the ringmaster.

_____ being quite far back, Agnes could see perfectly.

_____ the ringmaster had said 'Hello', the clowns came

bursting onto the stage. One had a large bucket of water which he

was throwing everywhere. _____ the people in the front

row were getting rather wet. _____, everybody was laughing

_____ they didn't mind a bit of water. _____ came the

acrobats. Agnes loved them, _____ the beautiful lady on the white

horse.

**B**    Put the connectives below into the correct category and then
make sentences using four of them.

**unlike    after    despite    also    as soon as    but    except**
**next    as well as    like    second    such as    finally**
**furthermore    too    in the same way    first    unless    yet    if**
**especially    so    on the other hand    because    thirdly    while**

Adding _____

Qualifying _____

Emphasising _____

Comparing _____

Contrasting _____

Sequencing _____

Illustrating _____

Cause and effect _____

_____
_____
_____
_____
_____
_____
_____
_____

**C** **Choose the correct connective to complete the sentence appropriately.**

**1** My friends and I all decided to walk to the swimming pool _____ (consequently/unlike/whereas) my brother waited for my dad to give him a lift there.

**2** _____ (in particular/like/in the same way) me, my brother has to get up early to catch the bus for school.

**3** My mother cooked the dinner _____ (as soon as/for example/next) she got back from work.

**4** Big dogs, _____ (therefore/such as/despite) mine, need a lot of exercise every day.

**5** I don't like drinking tea in the morning _____ (because/although/therefore) it makes me feel ill.

**6** I like to stay inside and read _____ (unlike/especially/unless) when it is wet and cold outside.

**7** I love apples _____ (as well as/moreover/except) bananas.

**8** I love all fruit _____ (as long as/except/too) bananas.

# For or against?

When we write an argument, we have to:
- decide whether we are **for** or **against** an idea
- present **opinions** clearly and in a **logical order**
- give **evidence** or tell a true story to support our point of view
- **persuade** the reader to accept our view.

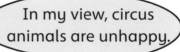

In my view, circus animals are unhappy.

1 Read these two letters to a newspaper. Which letter is for allowing animals to perform in a circus? Which letter is against?

2 Use the phrases in bold from the first letter to help you complete the second letter.

## Letter 1

**I am writing to express my** outrage that animals were performing at the circus in West Park. In my view, animals should not be allowed to perform in circuses.

Wild animals like elephants, monkeys and tigers should live in their natural habitat, which is the jungle. It was clear that the performing animals were unhappy. **For example**, the monkey seemed to be crying while it was rolling a hoop across the ring. **In my opinion**, we should set circus animals free.

Secondly, the trainers are beating the animals to make them do tricks. I know this fact because there was an elephant with a wound on its side while it was dancing. Its rider was hitting it with a stick in the very same place. **In addition**, the Animal Protection Society claims that three quarters of circus animals are cruelly treated.

**In conclusion**, if any readers are thinking of buying tickets for the circus next week, I urge them to think again. If you want to see wild animals, go to a wildlife park, not to a circus.

**Yours faithfully,**
J Gomez

## Letter 2

_____ support for allowing animals to perform in circuses. _____, animals love to please people and enjoy doing tricks.

Many of these animals were not born in the jungle but reared by loving trainers. They would not know how to survive in the jungle – they would probably get eaten by other animals. _____, some animals would not be alive if they were not in the circus.

_____, tigers are endangered because their jungle habitats are being cut down.

_____, there is no harm in keeping circus animals so long as their owners look after them properly.

_____

Kiran Grover

**B**  **Should children be television stars? Below is a list of arguments for (F) and against (A). Which are phrases for and which are against? Circle 'F' or 'A' to give your answer.**

**1**  Child stars grow up too fast. F/A

**2**  Child stars can earn a lot of money. F/A

**3**  They miss school, so get bad exam results. F/A

**4**  They often become stars in later life. F/A

**5**  They can become big-headed and greedy. F/A

**6**  They meet a lot of interesting people. F/A

**C**  **Write a letter to a newspaper arguing for or against allowing children to perform on TV and become television stars.**

_____

_____

_____

_____

_____

_____

_____

_____

# Using punctuation marks

## Colons, semicolons, dashes and brackets

**A** Put a colon in the appropriate place in the following sentences.

1 There are several items a well-equipped kitchen should have an oven, a sink, a fridge and a microwave.
2 I had been given a long list of things to buy at the supermarket milk, bread, apples, sugar, butter and flour.
3 If you are going on the camping trip there are several items you must bring a sleeping bag, a change of clothes, a torch, a plate, a dish and a cup.
4 Modern Art in the Twentieth Century The influence of Cubism

**B** Explain why the semicolon or colon is used wrongly in the following sentences.

1 I don't like him; not one little bit. _____
_____

2 After a long hard day at school; Raoul was ready for bed.
_____
_____

3 In 1985 the art world was rocked by a tragic event; the death of John Brown. _____
_____

4 Every school child must have: a bag, a pencil case, a pen, several pencils, a ruler and a rubber. _____
_____

**C** Write two sentences using a colon and two sentences using a semicolon.

_____
_____
_____
_____

# Self-assessment on my learning

## Unit 5 School days

Name _____

Date _____

😊 I understand and can do this well.

😐 I understand but I am not confident.

☹️ I don't understand and find this difficult.

| Learning objective | 😊 | 😐 | ☹️ |
|---|---|---|---|
| **Reading skills** | | | |
| I can understand how the author manipulates the reaction of a reader by using language of persuasion. I can recognise that a writer uses language to persuade a reader. I can use colons, semi-colons, dashes and brackets appropriately. | | | |
| **Writing skills** | | | |
| I can write an advertisement in an appropriate style. I can use connectives to structure my work. I can use a wide range of connectives. I can use the style of persuasive writing as a model for my own writing. | | | |

I would like more help with_____

_____

# Let's celebrate!

## It's Festival Time

A festival! A festival!

A friendly, family festival.

The time of year that's best of all.

A festival! A festival!

When food is most _____,

And games are all _____,

And presents are _____.

A festival! A festival!

A friendly, _____ festival.

A time of year that's _____.

A festival! A festival!

Sing songs and sound _____.

Religions east and west have all

got days they call a festival.

A festival, a festival!

A friendly, family festival.

The time of year that's best of all.

A festival! A festival!

## A

1 Complete the poem by adding one of the words/phrases below. Make sure what you write makes sense. Use a dictionary to look up any words you don't know.

**best of all      requestable      celestial      family      contestable      digestible**

2 One word isn't a real word. Which word has been made up by the author? Why?

_____

_____

3 "A friendly, family festival" What do you call the figurative technique that has been used in this sentence?

_____

## B

1 Write another verse to the poem by filling in the gaps with your own ideas. You can use the words below to help you. You might want to make up some words.

**animal  beautiful  carnival  credible  edible  extendable  flexible
delectable  plentiful  spectacle**

A festival! A festival!

When sweets are _____  _____,

And friends make a _____,

And laughter _____  _____.

2 Make one more verse, using the second verse as your model as you did in question 1.

_____

_____

_____

_____

Read your new poem to the class.

# Prefixes and suffixes

**A** Choose the correct ending from -able or -ible to complete the words below.

notice _____     vis _____     advis _____

accept _____     suit _____     terr _____

incred _____     like _____     horr _____

flex _____     bear _____     break _____

respons _____     avail _____

**B** The definitions below describe the name given to the people who do different professions. Write the name and choose the correct ending from -er or –or.

1  Someone who acts                                    _____actor_____

2  Someone who decorates houses          _____

3  Someone who works with law               _____

4  Someone who works on a farm             _____

5  Someone who works on a boat             _____

6  Someone who takes care of patients    _____

7  Someone who builds houses                 _____

8  Someone who visits someone else        _____

9  Someone who reports news                   _____

10  Someone who is in charge of money    _____

11  Someone who is in charge of a company  _____

12  Someone who marks exams                  _____

**C** **Find the following words hidden in the square.**

1 three words using the prefix, 'over-' _____ _____ _____ _____

2 three words using the prefix, 'mis-' _____ _____ _____

3 three words using the suffix, '-less' _____ _____ _____

4 three words using the suffix, '-ful' _____ _____ _____

5 three words using the prefix, 'fore-' _____ _____ _____

6 three words using the prefix, 'under-' _____ _____ _____

| f | o | r | e | w | a | r | n | i | n | g | s | l | u | o |
|---|---|---|---|---|---|---|---|---|---|---|---|---|---|---|
| o | v | l | o | v | e | r | c | r | a | m | o | e | n | v |
| r | e | e | v | f | o | r | e | t | o | l | d | s | d | e |
| e | r | s | e | l | g | f | o | r | m | l | e | s | s | r |
| s | a | s | r | u | e | f | e | c | k | l | e | s | s | d |
| t | l | y | p | f | l | e | s | s | o | o | m | e | e | o |
| a | l | a | a | s | h | a | r | m | f | u | l | l | l | n |
| l | s | l | i | s | m | i | s | f | i | r | e | e | e | e |
| l | u | r | d | i | c | a | r | e | f | u | l | g | r | s |
| e | n | e | o | l | e | s | s | f | u | l | u | a | a | s |
| s | n | d | p | b | a | s | h | f | u | l | l | u | c | u |
| s | e | n | o | d | s | i | m | i | s | g | u | i | d | e |
| s | i | u | n | d | e | r | c | o | o | k | p | e | n | n |
| s | n | o | w | h | e | n | w | o | r | g | r | e | d | n |
| u | n | d | e | r | a | g | e | n | t | m | i | s | a | i |

# Spellings

**A** **Choose the correct spelling to complete the sentences.**

1 You borrow books from a _____ .

library

libary

libury

2 Not all snake bites are _____ .

posernous

poisonous

poisernous

3 It was the most _____ film I've ever seen.

frighterning

frighterning

frightening

4 Can you _____ your dirty clothes so I can wash them.

seperate

separate

seperait

5 The comments she made were very _____ .

interesting

intresting

interesting

**B** **Correct the spelling mistakes in the following paragraph.**

The calinder showd it wos 6th June and it wos necessery for me to rember that it wood be my brofers berthday in free days time thyme. He wood be misrable if I didn't get him a precent so I desparately fought whot I coud get him wifout spending to much monee and came up with a marvollos idear – a humeros book culled Twelf nite by William Shakespeer.

**C** Complete the crossword.

**Across**

**4** The place you live in or stay at.

**7** Another word for the start of something i.e. a story.

**8** When you feel awkward, ashamed or self-conscious.

**9** The noun of strong.

**Down**

**1** Another word for occurred.

**2** This is how tall something is.

**3** The opposite of forget.

**4** When you have a disagreement.

**5** A homophone of 'court'.

**6** When something is needed, it is...

# Difficult words and homophones
## Spelling correctly

**A** Choose the correct homophone to complete the sentences.

**accept/except     desert/dessert     course/cause
saw/sore     mail/male     bald/bold     ate/eight**

1  I'm expecting a letter. Has the _____ been delivered yet?

2  I can't go to school today because I have a cold and my throat
   is _____ .

3  He hasn't got a single hair on his head. He is completely _____ .

4  Hannah could not _____ Diana's invitation as she was already
   busy that day.

5  "Who _____ all my sweets?" cried _____ year old
   Adam.

6  "You can't have _____ unless you finish your main
   _____ first," said her mother.

**B** Some of the following words have been mis-spelled. Write the
correct spelling next to any words that you think have the wrong
spelling.

definite _____          disapoint _____

embarress _____         nesessary _____

seperate _____          strenth _____

beatiful _____          dissapear _____

beggining _____         believe _____

**C** Rearrange the jumbled up letters below to create words which
are often spelt wrongly.

umreantg a _____        pomceellty c _____

ibsssune b _____        llnifay f _____

igmocn c _____          mariilaf f _____

# Self-assessment on my learning

## Unit 6 Let's celebrate!

Name _____

Date _____

☺ I understand and can do this well.

😐 I understand but I am not confident.

☹ I don't understand and find this difficult.

| Learning objective | ☺ | 😐 | ☹ |
|---|---|---|---|
| **Reading skills** | | | |
| I can use a poem as a model for my own writing.<br>I can recognise and understand different figurative language.<br>I can read and interpret poems.<br>I can recognise how poets play with words and their sounds. | | | |
| **Writing skills** | | | |
| I can spell words with unstressed vowels.<br>I can use prefixes and suffixes appropriately.<br>I can spell different words correctly, including homophones. | | | |

I would like more help with _____

_____

_____

_____

# Spies and mystery

## Using the mystery genre in writing
### Examining a writer's use of language

**A** Read another extract from *Stormbreaker* by Anthony Horowitz.

*Alex is in a metal scrap yard where they crush cars into small lumps of metal to reuse. He has taken his dead uncle's car there to be crushed but then he sees two men with guns coming in his direction.*

And then something hit the car with such force that Alex cried out, his whole body caught in a <u>massive</u> (_____) shock wave that <u>tore</u> (_____) him away from the steering-wheel and threw him helplessly into the back. At the same time, the roof <u>buckled</u> (_____) and three huge metal fingers tore through the skin of the car like a fork through an eggshell, trailing dust and sunlight. One of the fingers <u>grazed</u> (_____) the side of his head – any closer and it would have <u>cracked</u> (_____) his skull. Alex yelled as blood <u>trickled</u> (_____) over his eye. He tried to move, then was <u>jerked</u> (_____) back a second time as the car was <u>yanked</u> (_____) off the ground and <u>tilted</u> (_____) high in the air.

He couldn't see. He couldn't move. But his stomach <u>lurched</u> (_____) as the car swung in an arc, the metal <u>grinding</u> (_____) and the light <u>spinning</u> (_____). He had been picked up by the crane. It was going to put the car inside the crusher. With him inside.

**Replace each of the underlined words in the extract with a synonym listed below.**

**Make sure that the new word has the same meaning as the word it replaces and fits in the context of the sentence.**

| broken | bent | thrown | tipped | grating | huge |
|---|---|---|---|---|---|
| scraped | dripped | jumped | thrust | snatched | whirling |

**B** Using words and phrases from the passage answer the following questions.

**1** What threw Alex to the back of the car the first time? _____

_____

**2** Was it difficult for the machine to break through the metal of the car? Use words from the passage to explain your answer.

_____

_____

**3** Why was Alex thrown to the back of the car for a second time?

_____

**4** What made Alex's stomach uneasy?

_____

**5** Why was it crucial for Alex to leave the car as quickly as possible?

_____

**C** Look at the passage again.

**1** Write out examples of short sentences from the passage. What effect do they have? Why does the writer use short sentences sometimes?

_____

_____

_____

**2** Write out examples of powerful, descriptive verbs and adverbs used in the text.

_____

**3** Find an example of a simile in the text. What meaning does it express? Why did the writer use it?

_____

_____

_____

**4** Find an example of a metaphor in the text. What meaning does it express? Why did the writer use it?

_____

_____

# Word classes

**A** Put the words listed below into the correct category.

smelly   table   explode   yet   James Bond   running   bound   after   it
because   will   thoroughly   could   Africa   spoon   hidden   sneakily   nor
with   they   shouting   shrink   since   shuffling

common noun
_____
_____

past participle
_____
_____

adverbs
_____
_____

coordinating conjunctions
_____
_____

prepositions
_____
_____

personal pronouns
_____
_____

present participles
_____
_____

verbs
_____
_____

adjectives
_____
_____

subordinating connectives
_____
_____

proper noun
_____
_____

modal verbs
_____
_____

**B** Write six sentences which use two of the words from any of the word classes above.

*Example:* My old trainers were <u>thoroughly</u> <u>smelly</u>!

_____
_____
_____
_____
_____
_____

**Complete the table with the correct form of the verbs.**

| base form | past simple | past participle | 3rd person singular | gerund/present participle |
|---|---|---|---|---|
| became | | | becomes | |
| blow | blew | | | |
| catch | | caught | | |
| eat | | | eats | |
| forget | | | | forgetting |
| have | had | | | |
| lie | | | | |
| make | | made | | |
| put | | | | putting |
| see | | | | |
| swim | | | swims | |

# Relative clauses

**A** Rewrite the paragraph adding the correct punctuation.

**Spy Gadgets**

all spies use clever devices called gadgets in the james
bond movies the character 'Q' designs all the spy gadgets
he is based on a real man Charles fraser-smith who created
some of the most amazing gadgets during world war II

_____

_____

_____

**B** Read the paragraph and put all the verbs in brackets into the correct tenses.

**The past**

During the war, Fraser-Smith (think) _____ up ingenious solutions to difficult problems.
As a small compass (sew) _____ into clothes could (detect) _____, he (decide)
_____ to put magnetised needles inside matchsticks. The match could (drop) _____
in a pool of water and (point) _____ north, (act) _____ exactly like a compass.

**C** Add the missing connectives to the following paragraph.

**The future**

Gadgets _____ devices have become more important in spying. How we spy will change
in future _____ human agents can be easily seen _____ caught, _____
machines and gadgets can be made to destroy themselves _____ discovered. It also helps
that gadgets are very tiny _____ makes them harder to find. Nanotechnology is the name
_____ is given to the area of science _____ is to do with constructing microscopic
machines, called 'nanobats' _____ tiny robots. These could be sprinkled like dust over
electronic equipment _____ into rooms to send back information.

# Comprehension

**A** **Using words and phrases from the extracts on page 56 answer the following questions.**

**1** Who is the person that was the inspiration for the character of 'Q' in the James Bond movies?

_____

**2** What gadget was used instead of a compass?

_____

**3** Give two reasons why machines are more desirable for spying than humans.

_____

_____

**B** **What do you think?**

**1** Which gadget do you think is the most useful? Explain your answer.

_____

**2** In what way do you think gadgets will be very different in future?

_____

**3** Do you think there is such a thing as 'good' spying and 'bad' spying? Can you explain the difference?

_____

_____

**C** **What about you?**

**1** Imagine you have been asked to explain to a younger student what spying is. Write down what you would say to them.

_____

_____

_____

_____

_____

**2** Invent a new gadget for a spy. Prepare a speech and presentation to explain it to the class.

_____

_____

_____

_____

_____

_____

# Time connectives

**A** Find the following words hidden in the square.

| | | |
|---|---|---|
| after a while | in the end | soon |
| afterwards | later on | straightaway |
| at once | meanwhile | until then |
| before that | next time | whenever |
| next | previously | when |
| finally | since | |

| b | e | f | o | r | e | t | h | a | t | n | i | o | p | s | i | h | t | t | a |
|---|---|---|---|---|---|---|---|---|---|---|---|---|---|---|---|---|---|---|---|
| f | i | n | a | l | l | y | i | n | t | h | e | e | n | d | h | e | r | e | t |
| a | f | t | e | r | a | w | h | i | l | e | m | m | a | x | q | p | u | j | t |
| f | i | w | h | e | n | h | a | w | s | w | h | e | n | e | v | e | r | a | h |
| t | r | v | b | t | o | i | l | q | t | r | a | m | o | t | s | w | e | m | i |
| e | s | o | o | n | w | l | e | y | l | a | t | e | r | o | n | v | u | e | s |
| r | t | m | e | a | n | e | x | t | y | b | o | n | d | t | h | e | n | s | m |
| w | m | e | a | n | w | h | i | l | e | t | e | c | n | i | s | u | t | w | o |
| a | t | o | n | c | e | n | e | x | t | t | i | m | e | r | i | d | e | r | m |
| r | p | r | e | c | i | o | u | s | y | l | s | u | o | i | v | e | r | p | e |
| d | s | f | n | e | h | t | l | i | t | n | u | t | c | n | i | s | p | o | n |
| s | o | n | a | n | o | t | h | e | r | o | c | c | a | s | i | o | n | z | t |
| s | y | a | w | a | t | h | g | i | a | r | t | s | a | r | i | o | p | q | u |

**B** Write five sentences using a time connective.

_____

_____

_____

_____

_____

# Self-assessment on my learning

## Unit 7 Spies and mystery

Name _____

Date _____

☺ I understand and can do this well.

😐 I understand but I am not confident.

☹ I don't understand and find this difficult.

| Learning objective | ☺ | 😐 | ☹ |
|---|---|---|---|
| **Reading skills** | | | |
| I can sort words into their appropriate class. I can answer questions based on information in a text. I can analyse how a writer builds up tension. I can comment on a writer's use of English. | | | |
| **Writing skills** | | | |
| I can use connectives to structure my writing. I can use relative clauses successfully. I can use the correct punctuation in complex sentences. | | | |

I would like more help with _____

_____

_____

_____

# 8 Conserving our precious planet

## Reading and comprehension

### Saving our fish stocks

Read this interview with Angus McDonald, a marine expert and campaigner, fighting against over-fishing on the west coast of Scotland.

**Moira:** So, Angus, explain to us what over-fishing actually means.

**Angus:** Well, basically over-fishing takes place when the fish are caught at a faster rate than they are able to replace themselves. So numbers obviously <u>deplete</u>.

**Moira:** And this is what is happening off the west coast of Scotland?

**Angus:** This is what has been happening off the west coast of Scotland for many years now. The signs of over-fishing have been there since the 1980s and I warned the government over and over again that unless they brought in new <u>regulations</u> that made fishing here sustainable then it would have a <u>devastating</u> effect on the whole of the <u>marine</u> <u>ecosystem</u>. Now cod has been virtually <u>eliminated</u> from these waters.

**A** Look at the underlined specialist words in the text. Use your dictionary to match the words with a definition below.

1 Destroying, terrible effect _____

2 To remove or completely get rid of something _____

3 A law, rule or order made by authority _____

4 To decrease, lower in amount very seriously _____

5 A sea life system _____

**B** Underline the places in the passage above that help you answer these questions.

1 What is causing the decline of fish stocks off the west coast of Scotland?
2 What is Angus campaigning for the government to do now?
3 What does Angus think will happen if the government doesn't listen to him now?

# Prefixes

## Making words with prefixes

**A** Look at the meaning of the following prefixes.

**anti**: against  **de**: take away  **fore**: before  **mid**: middle

**mis**: wrongly  **non**: not  **over**: too much

**super**: above, higher than  **under**: under, too little

Using this information, explain what you think the *italic* words mean in the following.

**1** a can of *antifreeze* _____

**2** to *defrost* a window _____

**3** a weather *forecast* _____

**4** a *midseason* sale _____

**5** to be *misunderstood* _____

**6** a *non-smoking* area _____

**7** to feel you have *overeaten* after a meal _____

**8** to be a *superstar* _____

**9** for the meat to be *underdone* _____

**B** Add prefixes to the nouns in the list to form a word which matches the definitions below.

**wear**  **cover**  **coat**  **ground**  **act**  **cut**

**1** The place where the tube (electric train) runs beneath London. _____

**2** When you pretend to be someone you are not because you want to find out information. _____

**3** The clothes you wear under all your other clothes. _____

**4** The coat you wear on top of all other clothes. _____

**5** To offer something at a lower price than someone else. _____

**6** To act in an exaggerated way. _____

# Working on a passage

## Commas

 **Read the passage below and add commas where necessary.**

Recently a memorial was put up in the centre of my city to commemorate a man known as Snowy who worked relentlessly to raise money for animal charities. I remember Snowy also known as the 'mouse man' very well. As a child I would always drag my mother's arm as we got closer to the market in the town centre. Snowy had a long white curly beard and wore a top hat where his cat would usually be uncomfortably perched. His mice would scurry in and out of his pockets quite freely and the cat would never as much as look at them. Always dressed in bright colourful clothes Snowy was a gentle caring man who loved and was loved by all the local children. They would look at him in awe as he played all his musical instruments which included cymbals drums an accordion a harmonica and a recorder that were all somehow connected together so he could play them all at once!

## Writing instructions

 Write the instructions how to get from my house to Snowy's memorial. Instead of numbering the instructions, put a connective of order or sequence such as first, then, after that, finally.

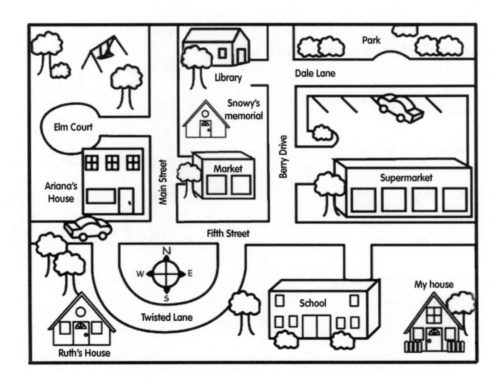

# Writing instructions

**A** Write the instructions for drawing a top hat like Snowy's. Write one instruction for each illustration. Add connectives of order and use adjectives telling how to do something (carefully, gently). Do not forget to add a heading and a list of materials needed.

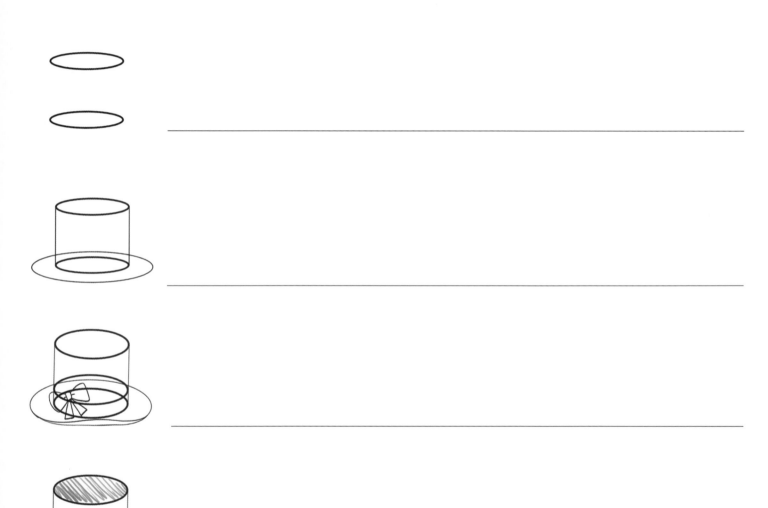

# The structure of a passage

## Linking paragraphs

 These sentences have been jumbled up. Put them in the right order. Give a heading and make three paragraphs with a subheading for each paragraph.

Larger <u>scale</u> avalanches happen when massive <u>slabs</u> of snow break loose from a mountain and travel down the slope at speeds up to 80 miles per hour in five seconds.

An avalanche can occur on any slope at any time if the conditions are right but most avalanches <u>occur</u> between December and April when there is a lot of snow.

Avalanches usually occur after heavy snowfall.

One of the worst effects of an avalanche is that it can clear a whole area of trees which then becomes an area <u>more prone to</u> avalanches in following years.

Many avalanches are just small slides of powdery snow moving down a slope as a formless mass.

An avalanche is the sudden <u>drastic</u> flow of snow down a hill or mountainside.

_____

_____

_____

_____

_____

_____

_____

_____

**B** **Using the information in the extract, answer these questions.**

**1** At what time of year is an avalanche most likely to happen? Why?

_____

**2** How fast can an avalanche travel?

_____

**3** What is the most common cause of an avalanche?

_____

**4** Do avalanches always occur after recent snowfall? How do you know?

_____

**5** What damage do some avalanches have on the environment?

_____

**C**

**1** Why is an area without trees more likely to have an avalanche than an area with trees?

_____

_____

**2** Why is there more likely to be an avalanche when there is an increase in temperature rather than a decrease?

_____

_____

**3** Is this text all facts, mainly facts or a mixture of facts and opinions?

_____

**4** Replace the underlined words in the extract with a synonym from the words or phrases below.

**happen**     **more likely to have**     **chunks**     **sized**     **forceful**

# Linking the heading and paragraphs in non-fiction text

## Studying fossils

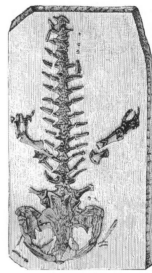

**A** Read this information extract. Then write a title and three appropriate subheadings for the extract in the spaces provided.

_____

_____

Would you like to work with objects that came from the Earth millions of years ago? That's what a palaeontologist does. A palaeontologist is a scientist who studies the animals and plants that existed on Earth a very long time ago. They mostly do this by studying fossils.

_____

Fossils are formed when an animal or plant dies and its body or form becomes trapped in sediment such as sand, mud or tiny pieces of rock. Over millions of years, this sediment is compressed or squeezed and buried under more and more layers of sediment. Eventually, it is compressed so much that it hardens into sedimentary rock with the fossil caught inside. Most fossils are found in sedimentary rock.

_____

There are two types of fossils formed from living things. There are vertebrate fossils which come from animals with bones and there are invertebrate fossils which come from plants and animals without bones.

**B** There are two main points in the third paragraph. Write them down, in note form, using as few words as possible.

**1** _____

_____

**2** _____

_____

# Self-assessment on my learning

## Unit 8 Conserving our precious planet

Name _____

Date _____

😊 I understand and can do this well.

😐 I understand but I am not confident.

☹ I don't understand and find this difficult.

| Learning objective | 😊 | 😐 | ☹ |
|---|---|---|---|
| **Reading skills** | | | |
| I can answer explicit questions using information from a text. I know what sort of language I should use in the different forms of non-chronological reports. I can discuss the language and grammatical features of different forms of non-chronological reports. I can compare the language and style of different forms of non-chronological reports. | | | |
| **Writing skills** | | | |
| I can write a range of different reports and adapt the text accordingly for the purpose. I can select the appropriate style for the reports I write. I can use paragraphs to sequence my work. I can write complex sentences and use the appropriate punctuation to mark out the subordinate clause from the main clause. I can use prefixes and suffixes appropriately to change the meaning of words. | | | |

I would like more help with _____

_____

_____

# A treasure trove of poems

## Making sense of the poem

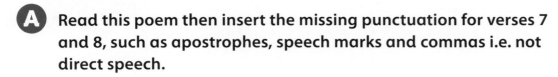

### Punctuation

**A** Read this poem then insert the missing punctuation for verses 7 and 8, such as apostrophes, speech marks and commas i.e. not direct speech.

**The ABC**

**1** 'Twas midnight in the schoolroom
And every desk was shut
When suddenly from the alphabet
Was heard a loud "Tut-Tut!"

**2** Said A to B, " I dont like C; His manners are a lack. For all I ever see of C Is a semi-circular back!"

**3** "I disagree," said D to B, "I've never found C so. From where I stand he seems to be An uncompleted O."

**4** C was vexed, "I'm much perplexed, You criticise my shape. I' m made like that, to help spell Cat And Cow and Cool and Cape."

Spike Milligan

**5** "He's right said E; said F "Whoopee!" Said G "'Ip, 'Ip, 'ooray!" "You're dropping me," roared H to G. "Don't do it please I pray."

**6** "Out of my way," LL said to K. "I'll make poor I look ILL." To stop this stunt J stood in front, And presto! ILL was JILL.

**7** U know said V that W Is twice the age of me. For as a Roman V is five Im half as young as he.

**8** X and Y yawned sleepily, Look at the time! they said. Lets all get off to beddy byes. They did, then "Z-z-z."

**B** Answer these questions about the poem.

**1** Why was D and B's understanding of C different? _____

_____

**2** Why does V say he is half of W's age? _____

_____

**3** Which letters of the alphabet were left out of the poem? _____

_____

# Kennings

**A** Match the kennings (1–12) with their definitions (a–l).

| | | | |
|---|---|---|---|
| **1** | bookworm | **a** | someone who knows what you're thinking |
| **2** | hot potato | **b** | the snow |
| **3** | mind reader | **c** | an environmentalist |
| **4** | rug rat | **d** | the ocean |
| **5** | showstopper | **e** | ice covered river |
| **6** | tree-hugger | **f** | a very popular performance |
| **7** | frozen road | **g** | a crawling baby or toddler |
| **8** | ship of night | **h** | poison |
| **9** | black cloak | **i** | something no one wants |
| **10** | winter's blanket | **j** | someone who reads a lot |
| **11** | dragon's bile | **k** | the moon |
| **12** | whale way | **l** | nightfall |

**B** Write your own kenning for each of the words/phrases listed below.

teacher _____

favourite game _____

homework _____

birthday _____

football _____

brother or sister _____

best friend _____

favourite food _____

school _____

music _____

**C** What creature is being described?

Treetop squawker
Loud screecher
Wing flapper
Colourful splendour
Show stopper
Jungle treasure

_____

# Direct speech

 **A** Use the sentences of dialogue below as a model. Explain the rules for how speech and dialogue should be punctuated and set out. There should be four rules.

She said, "Where did you find it?"
"In my house." He pointed without looking, because he was busy reading. "In the attic."
"What's it about?"
"School."
Margie was scornful. "School? What's there to write about school? I hate school."

_____

_____

_____

_____

**B** Below is an extract from *Earth is Room Enough,* by Isaac Asimov.

**Write out the lines and add in missing punctuation and reporting clauses, such as 'he said' and 'she shouted'.**

She read the book over his shoulder for a while, then said, "Anyway, they had a teacher
"Sure they had a teacher, but it wasn't a *regular* teacher. It was a man
A man? How could a man be a teacher"
"Well, he just told the boys and girls things and gave them homework and asked them questions
"A man isn't smart enough"
"Sure he is My father knows as much as my teacher."
"He cant A man can't know as much as a teacher.

_____

_____

_____

_____

_____

# Compound words

A compound word is created when two or more words are combined to create a new word.
*Example:* door + mat = doormat

**A** Match a word (1-10) with another word (a-j) to make a new compound word.

| | | | |
|---|---|---|---|
| **1** grand | | **a** keys | |
| **2** some | | **b** head | |
| **3** grass | | **c** mother | |
| **4** weather | | **d** end | |
| **5** house | | **e** thing | |
| **6** book | | **f** market | |
| **7** week | | **g** hopper | |
| **8** car | | **h** keeper | |
| **9** super | | **i** man | |
| **10** fore | | **j** case | |

**B** Add one word to each row to create new compound words.

*Example:* soup**spoon**   serving**spoon**   tea**spoon**   table**spoon**

| | | | |
|---|---|---|---|
| **a** ink _____ | flower _____ | tea _____ | jack _____ |
| **b** green _____ | tree _____ | light _____ | farm _____ |
| **c** horse _____ | dragon _____ | green _____ | house _____ |
| **d** sun _____ | moon _____ | day _____ | back _____ |
| **e** pen _____ | pocket _____ | fish _____ | jack _____ |

**C** Complete the following compound words by filling the gap with a part of the body. The first has been done for you.

*Example:* **ear**ache   **ear**phones   **ear**piece   **ear**wax

| | | | |
|---|---|---|---|
| **a** _____brush | _____ache | _____paste | _____pick |
| **b** _____liner | _____lash | _____brow | _____ball |
| **c** _____chair | _____pit | _____rest | _____lock |
| **d** _____ball | _____print | _____stools | _____path |
| **e** _____ache | _____band | _____rest | _____dress |
| **f** _____ball | _____bag | _____shake | _____print |

# Ups and downs

John Foster started to make up poems for his children to stop them from getting bored on long car journeys.

## The Price of Fame

It's not easy being famous.

Last week I was a hero.
In injury time

my namesake scored the winner
5   with a glancing header.

Everyone ran round the playground
chanting my name.

Today I'm a villain.
Last night I missed an open goal.
10  Then, just after half time,
I was sent off for a professional foul.
We lost two-nil.

Everyone's blaming me and calling me names.

If it goes on like this,
15  I'm going to ask Sir for a transfer.

John Foster

# Comprehension

**A** Give evidence from the poem to support your answers.

**1** Which line tells us how the player was treated as a hero? Which as a villain?

_____

**2** Which line within the poem tells us what this poem is really about?

_____

**3** The title of the poem is '*The Price of Fame*'. What alternative title would also give the reader an idea of what the poem is about?

_____

# Words, old and new

## Many common English words were originally adapted from other languages.

**A** Match each word (1-6) with the word it is related to (a-f).

| | | | |
|---|---|---|---|
| **1** quarrel | | **a** from the Chinese word kéjāp |
| **2** story | | **b** from the French word carotte |
| **3** hero | | **c** from the Latin word factum |
| **4** fact | | **d** from the Latin word historia |
| **5** carrot | | **e** from the Medieval word quadrellus |
| **6** ketchup | | **f** from the Greek word hérŏs |

**B** Match each word (1-9) with the the country of its origins (a-i).

| | | |
|---|---|---|
| **1** democracy | | **a** Italy (from concerto) |
| **2** homonym | | **b** Italy (from opera meaning work, action) |
| **3** telephone | | **c** Spain (from brisa meaning cold, northeast wind) |
| **4** feast | | **d** Greece (from demos meaning people) |
| **5** concert | | **e** Italy (from sŏlus meaning alone) |
| **6** opera | | **f** Spain (from huracān) |
| **7** solo | | **g** Greece (from homos meaning same) |
| **8** breeze | | **h** Greece (from phone meaning sound) |
| **9** hurricane | | **i** German (from fest with the same meaning) |

**C** Words that have changed meaning.

Choose five words from the list below and write two definitions for each. Write one definition of the word's present meaning and one definition of what it used to mean. Use a dictionary to help you.

artificial    brave    stupid    protest    last    hilarity    doom    bully

nervous    sad    pretty    guy    success    evil    nice    passenger

# Getting the spelling right

 **Circle the words with the correct spelling.**

public/publick    quic/quick     romantic/romantick    specific/specifick
basic/basick     tric/trick      candlestic/candlestick   critic/critick
logic/logick     panic/panick

 **Correct the spelling mistakes in the following sentences.**

**1** My brother set up a new bisness selling differant kinds of imported delicacies.

**2** Genarally, I find horror films very frightning.

**3** He gave a really genarous donation to the charity.

**4** Everybody sat at seperate tables.

**C** **Choose a word from below to complete the following sentences.**

**unique**      **smirk**      **wreck**

**1** The clothes he wore were completely _____ as he designed and made them himself.

**2** The diver found some ancient gold coins when he was searching the ship _____ deep down on the sea bed.

**3** He had a really smug _____ on his face when he told me that he didn't need my help as he had already done everything.

# Self-assessment on my learning

## Unit 9 A treasure trove of poems

Name _____

Date _____

😊 I understand and can do this well.

😐 I understand but I am not confident.

☹ I don't understand and find this difficult.

| Learning objective | 😊 | 😐 | ☹ |
|---|---|---|---|
| **Reading skills** | | | |
| I have read poems by different well-known poets.<br>I can answer questions about the ideas created in the poems.<br>I can spell and use compound words appropriately.<br>I know the origin of different words.<br>I know some meanings of words have changed over time. | | | |
| **Writing skills** | | | |
| I can use the correct spelling of 'k'.<br>I can punctuate my writing appropriately. | | | |

I would like more help with _____

_____

_____

_____

# Pulling together

**Oki was the** finest young hunter of his people.
He could run like the wind and carry great loads
on his back. He could pull fish from the coldest
sea, and there was no one who could paddle a kayak
5  with such speed and skill.

Oki's older sister was called Anuat. She was restless
and adventurous. She liked running out along the shore,
hunting small birds and taking them home to eat.

"I want to see life!" she used to say to Oki. "It's so dull
10  here at home. I want to meet other people and go to far
off places."

Oki's little sister was called Puja. She liked being at
home and helping her mother. They would cut up the
meat which Oki brought home, cook it and sew clothes
15  from the animal skins.

One winter's day, when the sea was quite frozen over,
Oki and the older sister, Anuat, went off over the ice
towards some distant islands.

"A fox! Look there! I'll catch him if I can!" shouted
20  Oki, and he raced away, as fast as a wind-blown bird.

The fox was fast, and the chase went on for many miles,
but at last Oki captured his prey. Pleased with himself, he
trudged back to the place where he had left his sister.

She wasn't there. He looked out over the frozen white
25  world and called as loudly as he could.

No one answered.

Then Oki saw marks in the snow. There were long
double stripes made by a sledge's runners, and between

them were the prints of reindeer hooves. All around, the
30   snow had been churned up, as if there had been a struggle.
   "What can this mean?" he puzzled. "Has my sister
been kidnapped? Why are there prints of reindeer hooves
between the marks of the sledge runners?"
   Baffled, Oki went home, hoping to find his sister
35   already there. But she hadn't returned. For days and days
the family waited and hoped, but Anuat never came back.
   Weeks passed, then months. No one talked about
Anuat any more, but she was in Oki's mind all the time.
   "I must find her. I must!" he said to himself.
40   Spring was coming now and the warm weather was
melting the ice between the islands. Oki gazed out across

the vast stretches of icy water. "If Anuat is still alive, she must be far away," he thought sadly.

But Oki was determined to find his sister. He thought
45  long and hard.

"When the sea freezes again, I will set out. But how can I avoid hunger and exhaustion? If only I could move more quickly over the ice."

Oki thought back to the reindeer prints between the
50  sledge marks. The seed of an idea planted itself in his mind. Was it possible? There was only one way to find out …

The next time that Oki went hunting, he took with him a sledge and some strong cords.

"Where are you going?" little Puja asked him. "What are
55  those cords for?"

"You'll see," said Oki, and off he ran, pulling the sledge after him.

It was days before he came home. From inside their snow house, Puja heard a strange noise. She ran outside to look
60  and screamed with fright.

"Father, Mother! Oki's come home, and he's brought a monster with him!"

Her parents ran to look.

"This isn't a monster," laughed Oki.
65  "It's a baby bear, and I'm going to train him to pull my sledge."

Oki's father shook his head and smiled at his son's folly. Oki didn't care. He made a harness for the little white bear and taught him to run
70  ahead of the sledge pulling it along behind him. But the bear cub tired quickly and soon lost interest. So off Oki went again.

A few days later, he came back. This time, unearthly howls brought Puja running out to look. She screamed
75 even louder than before.

"Look at its teeth, and its great round eyes, and its horrid bushy tail!"

"It's nothing to be scared of !" scolded Oki. "What a baby you are! It's only a wolf cub. Now let's see what he
80 can do."

Oki harnessed the bear cub and the wolf cub together, and tried to make them pull the sledge. But they fought each other, biting and scratching. They refused to make the sledge run at all.
85 Oki didn't give up. He made a special harness so that the two young animals couldn't reach each other. He petted them, and gave them good food, and at last he made them run together. But the wolf ran fast, and the bear ran slowly. The sledge went round in circles!
90 Oki tried again. He caught another wolf cub, and this time he trained all three to run together, with the bear in the middle. Now it was going well! Oki could ride on his sledge far and fast, and carry heavy loads, too.

\* \* \*

Winter came again. The sea was once more frozen
95 into a vast sheet of ice. The sun hung low in the sky, and
night fell almost before it was day. Oki made a new sledge,
stronger and faster than his old one.

"I'm going to look for my sister," he told his parents. "I
won't rest till I've found her."

100 His father and mother were worried.

"We've lost one of our children," they said. "How could
we bear to lose another? Stay at home, son. Forget your
sister. She is lost to us forever."

But Oki was determined. "I have my animals now
105 to help me," he said. "We can cover miles and miles in
one day."

He set off, racing fast to the place where he had last seen
his sister, out on the ice that covered the sea.

Soon, the bear was tired and slowed the others down, so
110 Oki unhitched him and carried him on the sledge.

Now, with the wolves alone, the sledge shot forwards, swishing across the ice faster than any person could run. On and on went the wolves, while Oki cracked his whip over their willing backs and shouted cries
115 of encouragement.

And so they crossed the sea, until at last they came to the far shore where the ground was rough and uneven. It was impossible to run the sledge over it.

Oki hitched his sledge to an iceberg and gave each of his
120 animals a big chunk of meat to eat. Then on he went on foot, alone. He was tired and hungry but he wouldn't turn back.

"I'll find you, Anuat. I'll find you!" he muttered to himself through the freezing wind that ruffled the fur
125 edging to his hood.

At last, he came to a settlement of igloos. A woman came out at his call. It was Anuat herself, and in her arms was a baby, all muffled up in fur.

"Oki!" she cried, her face lighting up with delight.
130 "How did you get here? How did you find me?"

He followed her into her igloo, and the brother and sister talked long into the night.

"That day," Anuat said, "when you ran off after the fox, some strangers came past. They snatched me up
135  and carried me away on their sledge. It was pulled by a reindeer, so we were soon far beyond anywhere I had been before. I fought and struggled, but they wouldn't let me go.

"Eventually we reached this land and I was forced to
140  stay. But then I met a good kind man here. We fell in love and married. Look, we have a baby now! There was only one thing that was making me unhappy, and that was the thought of my family, worried and wondering where I was.

"Now you have come all this way to find me! But how
145  did you do it, Oki? How did you come so far across the sea ice, on your own?"

"I'll show you in the morning, if you'll come down to the edge of the sea ice with me," said Oki, yawning. "But now, dear sister, I want something to eat. In fact, I
150  want a feast! So let me see what's in that pot bubbling so hard on the fire. I could eat a whole seal all by myself !"

And from that day to this, people have used the descendants of wolves to pull their sledges across the frozen Arctic landscapes.

*Elizabeth Laird*

# Word Cloud dictionary

## Aa

**aboard** *adverb, preposition* on a ship

**absorb** *verb* to take in, swallow or consume something

**accommodation** *noun* a place to live or stay

**actually** *adverb* really, in fact

**administration** *noun* controlling or managing something

**adventure** *noun* something exciting or interesting that you do, such as a journey

**aerodynamic** *adjective* designed to move well through the air

**Alaska native** *noun* a general term for the range of different people who originally come from and live in Alaska

**ancestor** *noun* a person who lived in the past and is related to people who are alive now

**anchor** *noun* a heavy metal weight that you drop into the water from a boat to stop the boat moving away

**ancient** *adjective* belonging to times that were long ago

**anemone** *noun* a sea creature that looks like a flower

**anniversary** *noun* a day when you remember something special that happened on the same date in an earlier year

**anticipation** *noun* the feeling of expectation or hope

**apps** *plural noun* software applications which can be downloaded onto multi-media devices

**archaeologist** *noun* a person who studies ancient civilizations

**architecture** *noun* the work of designing buildings

**argument** *noun* an angry disagreement

**Assalaam Alaikum** *idiom* greeting in Kazakhstan and other Muslim countries

**assignment** *noun* a piece of work that someone is given to do

**assisted** *verb* helped

**assure** *verb* tell someone something definite

## Bb

**backflip** *noun* a movement in, for example, gymnastics, when the body rotates backwards while in the air

**base on** *verb* use something as a starting point or foundation for something else

**beautiful** *adjective* very pleasant to look at

**beginning** *noun* the start of something

**believe** *verb* think that something is true

**bellow** *verb* act of emitting a loud, animal-like cry

**best interests (at heart)** *idiom* decisions based on what is for the best

**billow** *verb* rise up like waves on the sea

**blackmail** *verb* get money from a person by threatening to tell people something that they want to keep secret

**botanist** *noun* a person who studies plants

**bouquet** *noun* a bunch of flowers

**bowels of the earth** *idiom* deep under the ground

**breed** *verb* (of animals and birds) produce young ones

**bulging** *verb* sticking out or swelling

**bun** *noun* hair fastened in a small round shape at the back of someone's head

# Cc

**campaign** *noun* a planned series of actions to get people to become interested in something or to support you

**capable** *adjective* having the ability or capacity to do something well

**carnival** *noun* a festival or celebration with a procession of people in fancy dress

**cascading** *verb* like a waterfall

**cataclysm** *noun* a sudden violent disaster

**catch, caught** *verb* get hold of something that is coming towards you, such as a ball

**category** *noun* a set of similar sports, people or things

**cavern** *noun* a cave

**cavernous** *adjective* like a cavern i.e. a huge, deep, hollow area

**central nervous system** *noun* the system, consisting of the brain, spinal cord, and nerves, which sends electrical messages from one part of the body to another

**chant** *verb* call out words in a special rhythm

**chime** *noun* a set of bells or piece of metal which produces a musical sound when struck

**Chinese calendar** *noun* a Chinese calendar based on the cycles of the moon

**coach** *noun* a carriage pulled by horses

**coarse** *adjective* a coarse material has a rough surface or texture

**commemorate** *verb* when you commemorate a past event, you do something special so that people remember it

**commercial** *adjective* connected with buying and selling things

**common room** *noun* a room in a school or college where everybody can meet

**commotion** *noun* an agitated or noisy disturbance

**compulsory** *adjective* something which is forced, obligatory

**confectionery** *noun* sweets, chocolates and cakes

**conservation** *noun* the care and management of the natural environment

**conservationist** *noun* studies the protection and preservation of the environment and wildlife

**console** *verb* act of comforting or lessening the grief

**coral** *noun* a hard colourful substance made of the skeletons of tiny sea creatures

**Corroboree** *noun* a dance held by Aboriginal Australians at festival times or times of war

**courage** *noun* bravery, the ability to face danger, difficulty or pain, even when you are afraid

**crucial** *adjective* essential, of utmost importance

**custom** *noun* the usual traditional way of doing things, such as giving presents

# Dd

**damage** *verb, noun* injure or harm something

**dazed** *adjective* when you are dazed, you can't think or see clearly

**decoration** *noun* a thing that makes something more attractive or colourful

**definite** *adjective* fixed or certain

**delta** *noun* a triangular area at the mouth of a river where it spreads into branches

**desolate** *adjective* feeling or showing great unhappiness or loneliness

**dessert** *noun* fruit or a sweet food eaten at the end of a meal

**detect** *verb* notice something that is difficult to see

**diminish** *verb* to lower or decrease

**din** *noun* a loud noise

**direction** *noun* instruction to actors in a film or play

**disappear** *verb* when something disappears, it is impossible to see it

**disappointed** *adjective* sad after failing to do something, or after a hoped-for event has not happened

**dispute** *noun* an argument or disagreement

**discover** *verb* be the first person to find or find out something

**diver** *noun* someone who works under water using special breathing equipment

**downy** *adjective* covered in very soft feathers

**dream** *noun* something that you want for your life, such as an ideal or ambition

**Dreamtime** *noun* the set of beliefs of Aboriginal Australians

**dredge** *verb* drag something heavy along the bottom of the sea to scoop things up

**drought** *noun* a long period of dry weather

**drown** *verb* cover something in water

**dry-suit** *noun* a close-fitting, synthetic garment warn by divers to stay warm and dry

**duel** *noun* a prearranged combat between two people, fought with deadly weapons

# Ee

**ecosystem** *noun* a system formed by the interaction of organisms with the environment

**elementary** *adjective* basic or simple facts of a subject

**embarrass** *verb* make someone feel shy or awkward

**emerge** *verb* to come out from a place

**engineering** *noun* designing and building machines, roads, bridges and buildings

**entangle** *verb* get something caught up in a net or rope

**equality** *noun* the state of being equal, especially in status, rights or opportunities

**erosion** *noun* the process by which a surface is worn away by water/ glaciers/wind

**everything they are cracked up to be** *idiom* truly as good as people say

**evolve** *verb* develop gradually

**expedition** *noun* an organised journey or voyage made in order to do something

**excluded** *verb* ruled out, precluded

**exhale** *verb* to breath out

**expel** *verb* send somebody away from a school

**explore** *verb* travel around a place in order to find out more about it

**extinct** *adjective* an animal or bird is extinct when there are no more examples of it alive

**extra-curricular activities** *noun* activities outside school lessons

# Ff

**family tree** *noun* a diagram that shows all the people in a family

**famine** *noun* extreme scarcity/lack of food

**fault** *noun* a crack in the layers of rock of the earth's crust (between the earth's tectonic plates)

**feast** *noun* a large and splendid meal for a lot of people

**figure-skating** *noun* skating a series of movements and patterns on ice

**firecracker** *noun* a firework that makes a loud explosive noise

**firework** *noun* a cardboard tube containing chemicals that give off pretty sparks and lights and sometimes make loud noises

**flatter** *verb* to praise or compliment insincerely

**flipper** *noun* a limb that a seal or other water animal uses to swim

**float** *noun* a vehicle with a platform for carrying a display in a parade

**flood** *noun* a large amount of water spreading over a place that is usually dry

**flourish** *verb* grow strongly

**flutters** *verb* waves or flaps about, to flap the wings rapidly

**fly-on-the-wall** *idiom* imagining watching somebody without them knowing that you are there

**focused** *adjective* with very clear aims

**forsaken** *adjective* abandoned, deserted

**foul** *noun* an action that is against the rules of a game, such as football

**foundation** *noun* the groundwork, the support

**founder** *verb* to sink or fail

**freak** *noun* a very strange thing, animal or person

**free time** *noun* a period of time when you can do what you like

**frenzy** *noun* in a state of extreme agitation or wild excitement

# Gg

**gale** *noun* a very strong wind

**generation** *noun* a single stage in a family

**geologist** *noun* a person who studies the earth's crust and its layers

**girth** *noun* the measurement around something

**good cause** *idiom* a project that is worth supporting

**grounded** *adjective* if someone is grounded, they are not allowed out but have to stay at home

**gruelling** *adjective* a gruelling journey is one that is very hard and tiring

# Hh

**habitat** *noun* the place where an animal naturally lives

**half time** *noun* a short break in the middle of a game

**handlebar** *noun* a bar with a handle at each end, used to steer a sledge, bicycle or motor-bike

**happen** *verb* take place or occur

**hardtack** *noun* hard bread, like a biscuit

**harnessed** *verb* an arrangement of straps fastened to somebody or something

**harvest** *noun* the time when farmers gather the corn, fruit or vegetables that they have grown

**haze** *noun* when the sun is very hot it makes the outline of objects unclear

**header** *noun* the act of hitting the ball with your head in football

**heat** *noun* a preliminary round in a race or contest

**heave** *verb* lift or move something heavy

**height** *noun* how high someone or something is

**hero** *noun* a man or boy who has done something brave or important

**herring** *noun* an oily sea-fish about 30cm long that swims in large groups and is eaten as food

**hoarding** *noun* an advertising board in a public place

**hounder** *noun* a hunter

**hunched** *adjective* bent over and leaning forward

**hunter** *noun* a person who hunts animals or hunts for things

**hurricane** *noun* a severe storm with a very strong wind

**hurtling** *verb* rushing violently, with great speed

## Ii

**inappropriately** *adverb* to do something not right, not correct, not suitable

**incessant** *adjective* continuing without hesitation, unending

**indifferent** *adjective* having no particular interest or sympathy

**inquisitive** *adjective* to be interested and want to know about something

**in trust** *idiom* if money or property is in trust, there is a legal arrangement with instructions how the money or property can be used

**injury time** *noun* time added at the end of a football match because of the time lost while treating injured players

**inspector** *noun* a person who checks on a school and teachers

**interference** *noun* unwanted change or damage

**interviewee** *noun* (in an interview) the person who is being asked questions and asked to discuss something

**irrigation** *noun* the artificial application of water to land to aid crops

## Jj

**Jambo** *idiom* hello in Kiswahili, a language of Kenya

**Jericho** *noun* a famous ancient city

## Kk

**kayak** a canoe like boat

**keep an eye on** *idiom* watch a person or situation

**keeper** *noun* a person who keeps things, such as animals

**Konichiwa** *idiom* hello in Japanese

## Ll

**laden** *adjective* weighed down and heavy

**lagoon** *noun* a lake

**landslide** *noun* when a landslide happens, earth or rocks slide down the side of a hill

**languishes** *verb* lacking vitality and growing weak

**lasso** *noun* a long rope or line with a noose at the end used for roping horses or cattle

**leisurely** *adverb* without hurry

**lens** *noun* the curved piece of glass at the front of a camera

**lightning** *noun* a natural electrical flash in the sky

**litter** *noun* a number of young animals born at the same time

**locate** *verb* to purposefully find something

# Mm

**magnetise** *verb* turn into a magnet (a piece of metal that attracts iron and steel towards it)

**mandazi** *noun* a type of fried dough commonly eaten in Kenya

**marine** *adjective* to do with the sea

**marshland** *noun* a low-lying area of very wet ground

**medicinal** *adjective* to do with the treatment of diseases

**menacing** *adjective* something that threatens to cause evil, harm or damage

**microscopic** *adjective* not visible with the human eye; only seen through a microscope

**mock** *verb* to attack or treat with ridicule or contempt

**monsoon** *noun* the raining phase of changing weather patterns

**moon cake** *noun* a small cake traditionally eaten during the mid-autumn festivities in various parts of Asia

**mourning** *noun* the expression of sorrow for someone's death

**mud** *noun* wet soft earth

**multi-media** *noun* the use of sound, text and film as well as the printed word

**mutter** *verb* speak in a low voice

# Nn

**namesake** *noun* somebody with the same name as you

**necessary** *adjective* needed very much, essential

**needle** *verb* deliberately and continuously annoy someone

**nil** *noun* no score, such as in a football game

**nurture** *verb* to feed and protect something

# Oo

**obliged** *adjective* to feel compelled, forced or committed to something

**oceanographer** *noun* a person who studies the oceans

**origami** *noun* the Japanese art of folding paper to make attractive shapes

**overall pattern** *noun* the general way in which something is done

# Pp

**panic** *verb* be overcome with fear or anxiety and behave wildly

**paparazzi** *plural noun* (Italian) photographers who chase after celebrities

**papier-mâché** *noun* paper mixed with glue or flour and water, used for making ornaments

**papyrus** *noun* a kind of paper made from reeds

**parade** *noun* a line of people or vehicles moving forward through a place as a celebration

**parchment** *noun* an old-fashioned writing paper, sometimes made from goat-skin

**peer** *verb* look at something closely or with difficulty

**peer pressure** *noun* the influence of friends or colleague of the same age

**petite** *adjective* (French) very small

**physical exercise** *noun* exercises or sport that you do to keep your body healthy

**pilchard** *noun* a small sea-fish similar to a herring, eaten as food

**pinnace** *noun* a small boat, kept on a ship

**pioneer** *noun* one of the first people to go to a place or do something new

**pitcher** *noun* a container often with a handle and spout for pouring liquid

**plait** *noun* a length of hair with several strands twisted together

**playscript** *noun* the text for actors in a film or play

**play station game** *noun* a video game played on a special computer

**playground** *noun* a place out of doors where children can play

**pluck** *verb* remove something by pulling it quickly

**plumage** *noun* the entire feathers covering a bird

**prancing** *verb* leaping or dancing

**prehistoric** *adjective* from the time in history before events were written down

**preposterous** *adjective* a preposterous idea is completely unreasonable, or impossible to believe

**privileged** *adjective* having something special that only a few people have

**product** *noun* something that is made or produced for you to buy

**protest** *verb* say publicly that you think something is wrong

**prowling** *verb* act of creeping about in search of prey

**puffing** verb to blow out a short breath or send out smoke

# Qq

**quench** *verb* the act of satisfying (thirst, passion etc.)

**queue** *noun* a line of people or vehicles waiting for something

# Rr

**ragged** *adjective* irregular, uneven or broken

**raging** *adjective* continuing with great force or intensity

**ramp** *noun* a slope joining two different levels

**rattle** *noun* a rapid, short, sharp sound

**ravenous** *adjective* extremely hungry

**reality TV** *noun* a show where ordinary people take part

**recreational** *adjective* for relaxation and enjoyment

**recycling** *verb* to reuse something

**rein** *noun* a strap used by a rider to guide a horse

**remember** *verb* keep something in your mind, bring something into your
    mind when you need to

**replica** *noun* an exact copy

**resourceful** *adjective* clever at finding ways of doing things

**rhinoceros** *noun* a large heavy animal with one or two horns on its nose

**ridicule** *verb* to mock or tease, make something/someone look silly

**rowdy** *adjective* rough and disorderly behaviour

**rune** *noun* a letter of the alphabet used in the past by people in northern Europe

**runner** *noun* the part of a sledge that slides along snow or ice

# Ss

**saber (or sabre)** *noun* a sword

**safety harness** *noun* a combination of straps warn to keep wearer safe

**saltimbanco** *noun* street acrobat or entertainer; from the Italian saltare
    (jump) in banco (bench), which means to jump on a bench

**sawdust** *noun* a powder that comes from wood when it is cut with a saw

**scale** *noun* a single piece of skin that covers a fish, reptile or dragon

**scallop** *noun* a shellfish with two hinged fan-shaped shells

**scarper** *verb* to suddenly leave with great haste

**scientist** *noun* someone who studies science

**scooped** *verb* picked up or moved something

**score** *verb* get a goal in a game, such as football

**scramble** *verb* to climb or move quickly on rough terrain

**scurry** *verb* moving quickly

**scruffy** *adjective* untidy and dirty

**sea-fan** *noun* a fan-shaped sea creature

**seal** *noun* a furry sea animal that breeds on land

**seize** *verb* take hold of something or someone firmly or suddenly

**separate** *adjective* not together

**set one's sights on something** *idiom* decide that you want something
    and then try very hard to achieve it

**severe** *adjective* harsh or extreme

**shoulder** *noun* the part of your body between your neck and your arm

**shrill** *adjective* a high-pitch, piecing sound

**shrimp** *noun* a small shellfish, but sometimes used as an insult to mean 'little'

**siblings** *noun* brothers and sisters

**Sir** *noun* the formal name for a male teacher when talking about him, or to him

**skatepark** *noun* a place where people can do skateboarding and skating

**slammed** *verb* to shut with force

**sleek** *adjective* smooth and shiny

**sniffle** *verb* sniff repeatedly and noisily through your nose because you have a cold or are crying

**snoop** *verb*, *noun* try to find out about someone else's business; someone who does this

**snuffle** *verb* to draw air into the nose for the purpose of smelling something

**soar** *verb* to fly upwards

**social media** *noun* a collective term for communication by text, instant messaging, tweets, blogs, and email

**spatter** *verb* to splash with something in small particles

**species** *noun* a group of animals or birds that have similar features and can breed with each other

**speckled** *adjective* patterned with a small speck, spot or mark

**sphinx** *noun* a mythological creature from Ancient Egypt, with a human head and the body of a lion

**spine** *noun* the line of bones down the middle of your back

**splinter** *noun* a small sharp piece of wood or glass broken off a larger piece

**spoil** *verb* give a child everything they ask for in a way that has a bad effect on their behaviour

**sports day** *noun* a day at school when sports and games are played, usually outdoors

**squinting** *verb* to look at something with eyes partly closed

**starboard** *noun* the side of a ship or aircraft that is on the right when one is facing forward

**statue** *noun* a model made of stone to look like a person or animal

**stealthy** *adjective* careful and secretive

**strength** *noun* how strong a person or a thing is

**striking** *adjective* extraordinary

**stubborn** *adjective* fixed or unmoving in opinions or behaviour

**stunt** *noun* something daring or dangerous done as part of a performance

**suppress** *verb* contain, repress, dampen down

**surface** *noun* the top part of the Earth or a body of liquid, like water

**surge** *verb* move forward with power like an ocean wave

**suspicious** *adjective* to believe something is false, defective or guilty

**swollen** *adjective* description of something that has got larger like the waves of the sea or when a part of your body is injured

# Tt

**tablet** *noun* a flat piece of stone for writing on

**tax record** *noun* details of money that has been paid to the government

**tectonic** *adjective* to do with the Earth's surface, which is covered with moving tectonic plates

**tectonic force** *noun* the powerful movement of the layers (plates) that form the Earth's crust

**teller** *noun* a person who tells things, such as stories

**tempt** *verb* try to persuade someone to do something, especially something unwise

**the big league** *idiom* the most successful level in a sport

**the jury is still out** *idiom* people have not reached a conclusion yet

**tools of their trade** *idiom* work tools needed for their particular job

**toil** *verb* hard or exhausting work/labour

**to master s/th** *verb* to get the better of something

**topple** *verb* cause something to fall over

**tornado** *noun* a violent storm or whirlwind

**toss** *verb* is to throw or fling something

**track/field events** *noun* sports on a track or field, e.g. running, javelin, long jump etc.

**transfer** *noun* moving a player from one team to another

**trawler** *noun* a fishing boat that pulls a large net behind it

**trickle** *verb* move slowly like a thin line of water

**tumble** *verb* to fall down, head over heels

**Troy** *noun* a famous ancient city

**tsunami** *noun* a huge sea wave caused by an earthquake

# Uu

**uncontained** *adjective* something that cannot be kept or controlled

**uncover** *verb* to show or reveal

**unique** *adjective* something is unique when it is the only one of its kind

**unrivalled** *adjective* no equal

**up-to-the-minute** *adjective* fashionable, modern, the latest thing

# Vv

**vessel** *noun* a boat

**villain** *noun* a wicked or bad person, or a criminal

**violate** *verb* to disregard, abuse, defy something

**volcanic** *adjective* to do with a volcano (a mountain with a hole in the top formed by molten lava which has burst through the Earth's crust)

# Ww

**wail** *noun* a long mournful or sad cry usually high-pitch

**waterlogged** *adjective* if something is waterlogged, it is so wet that it cannot soak up any more water

**wattle** *noun* an Australian tree with a bright yellow flower

**wedged** *verb* forced into a narrow space

**willow** *noun* a type of tree

**wipe-out** *noun* (in surfing) a wipe-out happens when a big wave knocks you off your surfboard

**working a treat** *idiom* working very well

**worthy** *adjective* having great merit, character or value

**WWF** *noun* (World Wildlife Fund) the world's leading independent conservation organisation

# My vocabulary list

# My vocabulary list